STORIES FROM THE LIFE OF

JOSEPH SMITH

RICHARD E. TURLEY JR. & LAEL LITTKE

DESERET
BOOK

Cover illustration by Liz Lemon Swindle.

Interior illustrations by Robert T. Barrett.

Visit us at deseretbook.com

Library of Congress Cataloging-in-Publication Data

Turley, Richard E.

Stories from the life of Joseph Smith / Richard E. Turley, Jr., Lael Littke.

p. cm.

Includes bibliographical references.

ISBN 1-57008-915-9 (hardbound : alk. paper)

1. Smith, Joseph, 1805–1844—Juvenile literature. 2. Mormons—United States—Biography—Juvenile literature. 3. Church of Jesus Christ of Latter-day Saints—Presidents—Biography—Juvenile literature. 4. Mormon Church—Presidents—Biography—Juvenile literature. I. Littke, Lael. II. Title.

BX8695.S6T87 2003
289.3'092—dc21 2003000789

Printed in the United States of America 18961-7028
R. R. Donnelley and Sons, Crawfordsville, IN

10 9 8 7 6 5 4 3 2 1

Contents

PREFACE

Stories from the Life of Joseph Smith is a biography of the Prophet for young readers and others who enjoy a simple but dramatic presentation of events. It is divided into chapters of a comfortable length for bedtime reading.

The book closely follows genuine historical sources, filling in gaps where they exist and at times simplifying or creating dialogue to hold the reader's interest. Some quotations have also been simplified.

Where ambiguity exists in the historical sources, we have simply made choices in order to keep the narrative moving. We hope that readers of this book might later become interested in more serious Church history works that deal in greater detail with matters too complicated for this volume.

The book owes a great debt to the standard biographies and writings of Joseph Smith, his wife Emma, his mother, Lucy Mack Smith, and other early Church members, as well as to many other related studies by competent scholars. We wish to acknowledge this debt, even though we have consciously elected not to include source notes for fear of discouraging young readers.

Stories from the Life of Joseph Smith had its genesis in Richard's realization that he had no biography of the Prophet that he could recommend to his young children. We both hope this book fills that gap and will be enjoyed by many generations to come.

Richard E. Turley Jr.
Lael Littke

CHAPTER 1

A Dreaded Illness

When Joseph Smith, Junior, was born, no one on earth knew that someday he would be a prophet. Several years earlier, however, his grandfather Asael Smith had made a prediction. He said it had been made known to him that one of his descendants would do something that would change the world of religion. No one guessed it would be Joseph. He was just a boy growing up on a farm.

There is not much known about his early childhood. In a history of his life that he helped write as an adult, he hardly mentions his first few years. All he says is, "I was born in the year of our Lord one thousand eight hundred and five, on the twenty-third day of December, in the town of Sharon, Windsor county, state of Vermont."

Certainly he loved his family. Surely he enjoyed playing games with his older brothers, Alvin and Hyrum, and his older sister, Sophronia, and with the younger boys, Samuel and William.

He must have learned to work hard when he was still very young, because life on a farm meant everyone had chores to do. He would have grown familiar with animals, fences, fields, and orchards. Watching or working with his father and brothers, he would have begun early to learn farming, barrel-making, and other skills. Like most young boys, he was probably fond of sharp tools and had to be told to stay away from them, or taught to use them carefully.

When Joseph was five years old, his father, Joseph Senior, moved the family to Lebanon, New Hampshire. They all liked this new farm. One of the best things about it was that the children could go to school. Up until then they hadn't had much education other than what their parents taught them. But in Lebanon, Alvin, Sophronia, and Joseph, too, when he was old enough, could walk each day to a small school nearby. Hyrum was enrolled in a boys school connected to Dartmouth College in Hanover, a few miles away.

For a while, everything went well. The family was busy and happy. In July of 1812, a new baby girl arrived. They named her Katharine.

Then, in 1813, when Joseph was seven, there was an outbreak of typhoid fever. Thousands of people became ill, and many died. The Smiths hoped they wouldn't get it. But one day Sophronia said she didn't feel well. Hyrum came home from school with a high temperature. Both children were very tired and had red spots on their bodies. These were the symptoms of the dreaded disease.

As the days went by, Alvin and Joseph came down with the fever, too, then Samuel and William, and even baby Katharine. There wasn't much Mother Lucy could do to help them, except try to make them comfortable.

Eventually all of the children except Sophronia seemed to get well. Sophronia burned with fever and was so tired she didn't want to do anything but sleep. One day the doctor who took care of her drew Father Joseph and Mother Lucy aside and said, "There is nothing more I can do to prolong her life. The medicines will no longer help." After telling them to prepare for her death, he left.

That night Sophronia lay totally still. Her eyes were open, but she didn't appear to see anything. Mother Lucy refused even to consider that her little girl was going to die. "Please, Lord, let her get well," she prayed.

Deep into the night, she walked the floor, clutching the child to her chest.

The house was still as death, except for the sound of her footsteps. Then suddenly Sophronia sobbed. After another sob, she looked up into her mother's face and began breathing easily.

"She's going to be all right," Mother Lucy whispered gratefully.

Sophronia got well. But one morning Joseph felt a stabbing pain in his left shoulder. It was so bad that he cried out.

"Go get the doctor," Mother Lucy told Hyrum. "Hurry."

When the doctor came, he examined Joseph and said, "It will be all right, son. You've just sprained your shoulder somehow. Did you fall on it?"

Joseph shook his head. "No, it just began hurting all by itself."

The doctor insisted he had bumped it somehow. "But I'll do something to make it better," he said.

He put a small shovel in the fireplace to heat up while he rubbed liniment on the painful shoulder. When the metal of the shovel was hot, he held it against Joseph's shoulder. It wasn't quite hot enough to burn, but it hurt. Joseph tried not to cry. If it would make the ache go away, then he could stand it.

The trouble was that the pain didn't stop. As the days went by, it got worse. Then a large, ugly sore appeared under his arm. The doctor came and cut into the sore to drain it. "Now you will be well," he told Joseph.

But Joseph didn't get well. Instead, the pain shot like lightning down into his left leg and ankle. He pleaded with his parents to make it better. "It hurts so bad I can't bear it," he wailed.

To ease the pain, his mother carried him around in her arms until she was so exhausted that she got sick.

"Let me help," Hyrum said, and Mother Lucy gratefully let him take over.

For many days twelve-year-old Hyrum sat beside Joseph on a trundle bed, holding the aching leg between his hands. Joseph said that the pain wasn't as bad when Hyrum was there.

At the end of three weeks, Joseph was sicker than ever. His mother sent again for a doctor. A surgeon came and cut into Joseph's leg, making an eight-inch slice between his knee and his ankle to drain out the infection.

Joseph was so weak by now that he didn't care what they did, as long as the pain stopped. For a while it did stop, and Joseph was able to sleep peacefully for a few hours. But when the long incision began to heal, the pain came back. The leg swelled up, and Joseph again suffered from a blistering fever.

The surgeon returned and made another incision, this time cutting all the way to the bone. But it wasn't long until the leg began to swell again.

This time several doctors came to see Joseph, including Dr. Nathan Smith, who founded a medical school at Dartmouth College. He had devised a new treatment for the disease Joseph suffered from, and the other doctors had asked him to come. After they had all examined Joseph, they went into another room with his parents. Joseph heard them say a word he'd never heard before: *Amputation.*

"No," he heard his mother cry. "Can't you try something else?"

"No," one of the doctors said. "We can do nothing. The bone is so diseased that it is incurable. Amputation is absolutely necessary in order to save his life."

There was a long silence. Joseph lay quietly. *Amputation* must mean something terrible.

He couldn't hear his mother's words in reply, but her voice was firm.

The doctors and his parents came back into his room.

"My poor boy, we have come again," said one of the doctors.

"Yes," Joseph said. "I see you have. But you haven't come to cut off my leg, have you, sir?" Their faces were so serious that he guessed what *amputation* meant.

"No," said the doctor. "It is your mother's request that we should make one more effort. That's what we have come for."

Joseph whispered, "What are you going to do?"

The doctor cleared his throat. "Your mother has suggested that we cut into your leg again. Then we will take out the diseased part of the bone. This is a new treatment, but one I've tried many times, and we hope it will cure the sickness so that when it heals up again you will be well."

Joseph took a deep breath. "Then do it."

To his surprise, his father, who had hardly left his side, burst into tears. He sobbed just like little Samuel and William sometimes did.

Joseph reached out a hand. "It will be all right, Father."

The doctors began to bustle around, putting sharp instruments on a small table and covering them with a cloth so he couldn't see them. One of the doctors turned to Father Joseph. "Do you have some rope we can use to bind him?"

Joseph struggled to sit up. "No," he said. "No rope. I won't let you tie me."

The doctor said, "I'm sorry, son, but it will be painful. We must tie you down so you won't struggle."

"No," Joseph repeated.

In those days, they did not have good medicine for pain. So the doctor said, "We will give you some liquor. You must take something. Otherwise you cannot endure the operation."

"No." Joseph shook his head. "No. I don't want anything. Father will hold me." He gripped his father's hand. "That's all I need."

The doctors talked with one another for a moment, then said they would try it that way.

Mother Lucy bent over Joseph. "I'll be here, too, son," she said.

She looked so pale that he feared she might faint. He thought about the many days she had carried him around until she was ill herself.

"Mother," he said. "Please go outside. I don't want you to watch."

She knelt beside his bed, putting her arms around him. "I have to help you through it."

"No," Joseph said. "You've done enough already. Father is here, and the Lord will bless me. He made Sophronia well. He will help me, too."

Tearfully his mother nodded. She brought a pile of folded sheets to put under his leg, kissed him softly, and left the room.

The operation began. All Joseph could remember later was a blur of terrible pain. At times there was nothing he could do but cling tightly to his father and cry out. When the doctors started taking out the bad pieces of the leg bone, he screamed so terribly that his mother burst into the room.

"Oh, my poor boy," she cried in a trembling voice. "Let me stay with you."

"Go back, Mother," he said with all the strength he had left. "Go back outside."

Reluctantly she left. The doctors went on operating. They removed nine pieces of bone from Joseph's leg. His father stayed with him through it all, whispering encouragement and sometimes singing in his ear, and praying.

The operation was successful. Much of the pain was gone. But before the leg healed, fourteen more pieces of bone came out. Joseph was still very ill. He got so thin that his mother could easily carry him around like a baby. When he wasn't being carried, he had to either stay in bed or use crutches to help him hobble around.

Eventually the leg improved, but Joseph always had a big scar and limped slightly for the rest of his life.

It was a terrible experience for Joseph to endure, but it made him strong and helped prepare him for other difficulties to come.

CHAPTER 2

MOVING WESTWARD

The time of sickness was over, but now there were more bad times for the Smith family. Instead of being able to save money for the future, they had to spend a lot to pay the doctors and just to survive while their health improved. After settling their debts, the Smiths had very little for themselves.

Father Joseph decided they could make more money if they moved to a village named Norwich, back in Vermont. But things did not go well there, either. The first year their main crops failed, and they lived on what they were able to harvest from the orchard and garden, plus what they could get by trading with neighbors. Sometimes Father Joseph and Alvin were able to find work that brought in a little money.

The second season the crops failed again.

Father Joseph told the family they would stay one more year in Norwich. But if the crops failed yet again, they would move to New York, where wheat grew well in the fertile soil. Moving was always hard. But so was trying to live on a farm without good crops. Everyone felt that wherever they went would be all right as long as they were together.

The next year, 1816, became known as "the year without a summer," partly because of something that had happened in Indonesia, on the other side of the world. A volcano named Mount Tambora had erupted in 1815, killing more than 10,000 people. It spewed so much dust and ash into the air that the sky was dark for three days. High in the sky, the winds picked up the dust and ash and blew them all around the world. These blocked some of the sunlight from reaching the earth. Temperatures dropped so low in New England that snow fell in the summer and ice formed on rivers and ponds. It was so cold that the crops did not grow well.

There was one joyful event that year—the birth of a new baby named Don Carlos. But as the summer came and the harvest was poor again, things did not look good for the Smiths.

One day Father Joseph came home in a very somber mood. He sat in a chair and thought to himself for a long time. Finally, he spoke. "Well, I've decided to go to western New York. It's just a matter of how soon. I read in the newspaper about land selling there for $2 to $3 an acre. The article said it's very fertile, good for raising crops. Mr. Howard is headed that way, and I'd really like to go with him and take a look at it."

New York! Joseph, who would soon be eleven, had thought about moving there ever since Father had first mentioned it some time ago. Then it was just an idea. Now it was real. Joseph wasn't sure just how far away New York was, but he knew it would mean several days of travel.

For a young farm boy of his day, he had already traveled a lot. Besides moving with his family, he had gone on a long trip with his Uncle Jesse to Salem, Massachusetts, by the Atlantic Ocean. His parents had thought the sea breezes would help him get better after his leg operation, and they did. He had enjoyed Salem, and now they were going to the state of New York!

"When will we leave?" he wondered. He listened carefully as his parents talked and soon heard answers to all his questions.

"It's over 300 miles," Father said, "but the sooner we get there, the sooner we can get settled and start a new life together."

"Then you'd better leave right away and find a place for us to live," Mother

Lucy said. "We can't stay here. People are starving, after three years without a good harvest."

Father Joseph gazed around at his family. "But," he said, "how can I leave right now? You couldn't get along without me. Besides, I still have some debts. I can't go as long as I owe money to anyone."

Mother Lucy urged him to figure out just how much money they could put together to pay the debts. "Also," she said, "there are people who owe money to you. Perhaps you could ask them to pay the people you owe money to. That way the debts will be paid."

"That might work," Father Joseph said. "But how will you get along if I leave you here alone?"

"Alone?" Mother Lucy raised her eyebrows. "I have eight children here with me. Alvin is eighteen now, and Hyrum sixteen. They are both husky boys and work hard. Sophronia is thirteen and a great help with the younger children."

"But there's Joseph," Father Joseph said. "He's still on crutches."

"I can help, Father," Joseph insisted. "And I'll be able to travel just fine when it's time for us to go."

"We have to go somewhere, Father," Alvin said. "We can't make a living here anymore."

Father Joseph thought for a while, then said, "All right. I'll see what I can do about the debts."

In the next few days he did as Mother Lucy had suggested. As soon as all the arrangements were made, Mr. Howard came by, and he and Father left together for Palmyra, New York. Alvin and Hyrum followed along the road with their father for some distance before turning back. Joseph, standing with his crutches, watched from the house. They all knew that life on the farm would not be easy with Father away.

Mother Lucy and the children worked hard to live and to prepare for the move. Although Joseph's leg was still painful, he did his part. Grandmother Lydia Mack, Mother Lucy's mother, came to help with baby Don Carlos and the other small children.

After many weeks, Mother Lucy received a letter saying Father Joseph had sent a team of horses and a wagon to take them to New York. When the wagon arrived, it was driven by Caleb Howard, the cousin of Father Joseph's traveling companion. The family loaded up their belongings and said good-bye to their neighbors. Three hundred miles was a long distance, and they would not see some of them again.

But now there was more trouble. Some of the men with whom Father Joseph had settled debts insisted they had not been paid. They said the Smiths could not leave until the debts, which they claimed amounted to $150, were taken care of.

Several friends of the family said they would help Mother Lucy prove that the money had indeed been paid. The friends also said they would take up a collection for her. But Mother Lucy knew her friends were struggling too and did not want them to give up their hard-earned money. She gathered her family together to discuss what to do about the debts.

She reminded them that they needed to leave right away, since Mr. Howard was waiting for them. It would take a long time, maybe even weeks, to gather all the proof they would need to show that the debts had already been paid.

They finally decided that they would just pay the debts again so they could get started on their long journey. They put together all of the cash they had and sold some of their household things. They were able to raise the necessary $150, but that left very little money for the trip.

By that time, the snow was deep, and they had to travel the first part of the journey by sleigh. When the sleigh was loaded, everyone dressed in the warm woolen clothes Mother Lucy and Grandmother Mack had prepared and set off on this new journey. In the weeks since Father Joseph had left, the weather had grown quite cold.

They hadn't gone very far when the sleigh overturned, and Grandmother Mack was injured. When they reached Royalton, where Grandmother was planning to stay with her son, they had a tearful parting. Grandmother cried and said she would probably never see any of them again. "I have lived long," she said. "My days are numbered."

"No, Grandmother," Joseph and the other children cried. "You will be all right."

She shook her head and continued speaking. "I must soon exchange the things of this world for another state of existence. I beseech you to continue faithful in the service of God to the end of your days, that I may have the pleasure of embracing you in a fairer world above."

She asked them all to kiss her good-bye. Then, with her words echoing in their ears, the family started again toward New York, changing from the sleigh to a wagon.

Very soon there was still more trouble. This time it was with Caleb Howard, the man who drove the wagon. Father Joseph had paid Mr. Howard ahead of time to drive the family to Palmyra. Mr. Howard chose to spend the money on liquor and gambling as they went along. He was also cruel.

In those days, people often walked next to their wagons when they moved. The wagons carried the belongings and those who couldn't walk well or chose to ride. Still on crutches, Joseph was allowed to ride at first.

Then Mr. Howard got friendly with two girls from the Gates family, which was traveling in sleighs along the same road. Mr. Howard asked the Gates girls to ride in the wagon with him instead of Joseph. He made Joseph get out and walk in the snow with the others for many miles each day.

Joseph's brothers pleaded with Mr. Howard to let Joseph ride because his leg still hurt and it was hard for him to walk. But Mr. Howard got so angry at their request that he knocked the boys down with a whip.

"I can walk," Joseph said, although his pain showed on his face. "Let's go on."

Reluctantly his brothers agreed to let him continue stumbling along behind the wagon.

One morning after they had stayed the night at an inn, Alvin came running with terrible news. "Mother," he said, "Mr. Howard has thrown our goods out of the wagon and is starting off with the team."

In those days, people often walked next to their wagons when they moved.

Mother Lucy was busy getting the baby and smaller children ready to travel. "Go stop him," she told Alvin. "Tell him I must see him. Bring him into the inn."

Alvin hurried back outside. Soon he returned with Mr. Howard, who scowled at them. "Why do you stop me?" he snarled at Mother Lucy. "The money your husband gave me is gone. I'm not hauling you any farther. I'm taking my team and wagon and getting out of here."

Joseph wondered what his mother would do. He watched her straighten her back. With the baby in her arms, she walked up to Mr. Howard. She looked very small beside him. She stared fiercely up at him for a moment, then turned to the other people there at the inn.

"Gentlemen and ladies," she said loudly enough so that everyone could hear. "Please give me your attention. Now, as sure as there is a God in heaven, that team and wagon belong to my husband. This man intends to take them from me, leaving me with eight children and no way to go on with my journey."

Turning to look up again at Mr. Howard, she said, "Sir, I forbid you to touch the team or drive it one step farther. You can go about your business. I shall hereafter attend to my own affairs."

The crowd of people cheered, and Mr. Howard left the inn. Mother Lucy followed him, grabbing the horses by the reins to make sure he didn't run off with them. Seeing the crowd of witnesses, Mr. Howard stopped trying to steal the wagon and slunk away.

Joseph was very proud of his mother. He and Alvin and Hyrum stacked the goods back in the wagon while she finished getting the younger children ready. They found that Mr. Howard had lost or traded away some of their belongings. Even worse, they had scarcely any money left. But they still had one another.

When everything was ready, Mother Lucy handed the reins to Alvin. "You'll be our new driver," she directed. She arranged for young Joseph to ride in one of the comfortable sleighs driven by a son of the Gates family. Taking the baby from Sophronia, Mother Lucy drew a deep breath and looked down the icy road to Palmyra. "Come on, children," she said. "We're going on."

CHAPTER 3

THE FIRST VISION

As they continued their journey, Mother Lucy paid for their food and lodging by selling cloth she had brought along to make clothing for the family. When that was gone, she sold any extra clothes they had. She paid the last bill with a pair of earrings that Sophronia took from her ears. Sophronia felt sad about giving up her earrings but was comforted because now it was possible for the family to keep traveling on.

By the time the wagon rolled into Palmyra, they had two cents left. Father Joseph had been watching for them and came out to meet their wagon. The members of the family had a joyful reunion.

"Where's Joseph?" his father asked.

"He'll be along soon," Mother Lucy replied. But when the sleigh that Joseph had been riding in pulled up, Joseph wasn't in it.

"What happened to Joseph?" Mother Lucy asked, astonished. The driver shrugged his shoulders. He said Joseph hadn't been with them for many miles. He drove on, leaving everyone in the family anxious and concerned for young Joseph.

"What are we going to do?" Lucy asked her husband.

"Let's get the other children inside first," he answered. Father Joseph took them into their new home, a little house on the west end of Main Street. As the other children settled in, Mother and Father talked seriously about how to find their lost boy.

But before long, Joseph found them. A wagon stopped in front of the house. He was in it. He had been bleeding. His parents ran out to meet him.

"What happened?" they asked.

"This morning," Joseph said in a shaky voice, "I went to get in the sleigh. The driver looked around to see if anyone was watching. Then he knocked me down and made me bleed. He took off without me. After a while, this man picked me up."

Joseph and his parents thanked the nice man in the wagon for his kindness. Then the whole family gathered inside the house and enjoyed a meal together. The journey had been long and cold. They were happy to relax and warm themselves, and especially to be all together again.

As they rested, Mother Lucy and the children told Father all about what had happened back in Vermont and what Mr. Howard had done.

"There are many bad people in the world," Father Joseph said. "But we won't let them hold us back. Let us just think of our new life here in Palmyra."

It was a happy life, even though they were very poor at first. They decided they would all work hard so they could someday buy a big piece of land. All of Joseph's life, the family had rented other people's land to farm. They dreamed of having a farm of their own.

Joseph, who turned eleven in December, didn't have much chance for schooling. He attended a small log schoolhouse nearby for a short time to study reading, arithmetic, spelling, and grammar. He was also taught at home by his mother and father, both excellent teachers. But when the weather was warm enough, he did his part to help earn money for the family.

Father Joseph, Alvin, and Hyrum worked for other people to bring in much-needed cash. They cleared the people's land and planted, tended, and harvested their crops. They built stone walls, dug wells, and made barrels. The family opened a shop at the east end of the village, where they sold cakes and root beer. Mother Lucy kept house and painted oilcloth to sell. Sophronia helped her around the house, and Joseph worked wherever he could.

Father Joseph built a cart that Joseph used to sell tasty goodies around town, especially on celebration days when there were many people about. In those days, when young men turned eighteen, they had to join the militia, a part-time citizen army. When they practiced their marching and drills, people came from miles around to watch. Alvin and Hyrum joined the militia and practiced with it. Joseph, who was proud of them, helped earn money by selling food from his cart to the people who came to watch.

The Smiths finally found some land they wanted to buy two miles south of the village. It was large and had lots of trees. In 1818, they were allowed to start working on it. They also rented a piece of land next to it. Their neighbors and friends helped them build a nice log home.

The house had a ground-floor kitchen with a brick fireplace and another room for entertaining in which Mother and Father would sleep. Upstairs were two rooms where the children slept. The home was neatly furnished with wooden furniture built by Father Joseph, as well as things Mother Lucy bought with the money she earned.

Joseph helped his father and older brothers clear the trees off the land they were buying. As time went on, Joseph grew tall and strong and was able to work like a man even though he was still a boy. His friendly, cheerful personality made him popular with the other young people in the area. He joined in house and barn raisings, corn huskings, and athletic contests. He went hunting and trapping, enjoyed dances and parties, and was active in a debating group.

In the winter, Father Joseph and his boys cut down trees and cleared the land, skidding the logs along the frozen ground. They split many of the logs to make fence rails. When the weather warmed, they planted crops. The first year they cleared thirty acres and built fences. Over time, they cleared more land, added more fences, raised a barn, and planted an apple orchard.

When they weren't working on the farm, Father Joseph and the boys helped other farmers. They also brought in extra money by making barrels, chairs, baskets, and birch brooms. Their neighbors called them honest, hard-working people.

Palmyra was a thriving, bustling village of about 600 inhabitants at that time. Many more people lived on surrounding farms. The soil, once it was cleared of trees, was as fertile as the advertisements had said it was. Besides being good for raising wheat and corn, it produced fine orchards of apples, pears, cherries, and peaches. Berries grew in the forests, and fish could be caught in the streams. The Smiths were grateful to eat well after experiencing hard times in their old home.

At this time there was an unusual excitement in the area about religion. People were enthusiastic about spiritual matters. They listened to the various preachers compete for followers. Each one told why his particular church was the right one.

Joseph's family had always been religious. They had always had family prayers. Father Joseph had a habit of carrying his spectacles in his vest pocket, and when Joseph and the other children saw him pull them out and perch them on his nose, they knew they should get ready for prayer and reading the Bible.

Mother Lucy and some of the children had thought about joining a church back in Vermont and New Hampshire. But because they moved around a lot and there was always so much work to be done, they had never gotten around to it. Now, after they listened to the various preachers, Lucy, Hyrum, Samuel, and Sophronia joined one of the churches. Joseph wanted to join a church too, but he couldn't decide for sure which one.

He searched the scriptures to learn about the word of God. But when he thought of wicked, cruel men like those back in Vermont who had made Mother Lucy pay the family debts twice, or like Mr. Howard, Joseph realized that people did not live up to what the scriptures taught. This made him question what the various preachers said. He couldn't make up his mind who was right and who was wrong. But he considered it very important because whatever choice he made would have eternal consequences.

For months, Joseph thought a lot about the various religions as he helped his father and brothers plow the fields, dig wells, hoe corn, and cut up trees for firewood. The more he thought, the more confused he became.

He believed firmly in God and saw evidence of Him everywhere he looked–in the sun shining above, the moon floating across the sky, the stars glowing in the night, and the earth on which he stood. He could see God's work in the animals, birds, and fish that lived near his home.

In the summer of 1819, one church had a camp meeting down the road some distance from the Smiths. It lasted for days, and Joseph pulled his cart there to sell baked goods. He enjoyed listening to the preaching, but still couldn't decide which church he should join.

Through the fall and winter, he continued to think and to study the family Bible. His search of the scriptures did not lead him to any particular church. None of them seemed to be built upon the gospel of Jesus Christ as he understood it from the New Testament. He began to feel sad for the bad things some people did. He also felt sorry for his own mistakes.

About this time a strange thing happened. Joseph, who was now fourteen, was on his way home from an errand. As he crossed the yard, he heard a gunshot. A lead ball whined so close that he felt someone was trying to kill him. Frightened, he ran into the house, breathlessly telling his family about the shot. They hurried outside but could find no trace of the gunman. The next morning they found tracks under a wagon. They also found that one of their cows had gunshot wounds in her head and neck. They never found either the person who had fired the gun or the reasons why he had done so. It did not happen again.

Joseph continued to ponder which was the right church to join. What should he do? Which of all the religions was right? Or were they all wrong? How would he know?

One day in the early spring of 1820, when he was reading the New Testament, he came across James 1:5, a verse that caught his attention. It said, "If any of you lack wisdom, let him ask of God, that giveth to all men liberally, and upbraideth not; and it shall be given him."

The words impressed him deeply. He read them over and over.

He finally decided that if he was ever to get an answer to his questions about which church was right, he needed to do what James said: Ask God.

He knew where he would go. There was a quiet, peaceful grove of trees near his home, and in the grove was a clearing. He had been working there earlier and had left his axe in a stump. It would be a good place to pray.

When he reached the clearing, he looked around to make sure there was no one else nearby. He had never prayed aloud before, and he didn't want anybody listening.

Satisfied that he was alone, he knelt down and began to pray out loud. He had scarcely begun when he was seized by a strange power. It bound his tongue so he couldn't speak. Thick darkness gathered around him. His heart pounded, and he felt that he was surely doomed to destruction. He struggled against the power, using all his strength to plead with God for help. But it didn't seem as if help would come.

Just when Joseph was about to give up, he saw a pillar of light exactly over his head. It was brighter than the sun, and as soon as it appeared, the evil power released him.

Gradually the light descended toward him, increasing in brightness. By the time it reached the tops of the trees, the grove for some distance around was brilliantly lit. Joseph expected to see the trees burst into flames as soon as the light touched them. When they didn't, he felt he could endure the light too.

It continued to come down, slowly, slowly, until it rested upon the earth, with him in the midst of it. As the light fell on him, Joseph saw two beings, gloriously bright beyond description. They stood in the air above him. "Joseph," said one of them, pointing to the other. "This is my Beloved Son. Hear Him."

Joseph knew beyond a doubt that these beings were God the Father and His Son, Jesus Christ. Weak and trembling, he tried to gather his thoughts together. He had come to ask for wisdom. He had not expected his fervent prayer to be answered in this way.

Satisfied that he was alone, Joseph knelt down and began to pray out loud.

As soon as he could, he stammered out his question. "Which is the right church? Which should I join?"

He was told to join none of them. Jesus spoke, saying, "The churches draw near to me with their lips, but their hearts are far from me." He said He was about to restore His true Church to the earth with the fulness of the gospel. Joseph, He said, would assist in the work, if he was obedient. Joseph wondered about his worthiness.

"Joseph, my son, thy sins are forgiven thee," Jesus said. "Go thy way. Walk in my statutes and keep my commandments. Behold, I am the Lord of glory. I was crucified for the world, that all those who believe on my name may have eternal life."

Jesus talked to Joseph for some time. Then the vision faded and Joseph found himself lying quietly on the ground, filled with a sense of wonder.

Chapter 4

An Angel in the Night

Joseph lay on his back on the ground for several minutes after the brilliant light dimmed and disappeared. He was amazed at what he had seen, but he also felt weak. Had he really seen two glorious Personages standing there in the radiance?

He knew he had. There was no mistaking what he had seen. Nor what he had heard.

He took several deep breaths, and then attempted to rise to his feet. Although his legs were trembling, he found that he could walk. Slowly he made his way across the fields to the house. Mother Lucy was there at the table, mending a pair of breeches. She greeted him cheerfully.

Joseph merely nodded to her. Then the weakness returned, and he leaned against the fireplace.

Mother Lucy looked concerned. "Joseph, are you all right?"

He shook his head. "Never mind, all is well," he said. "I am well enough."

He didn't say anything about his astounding experience except to tell her that it had been made known to him that the church she had joined was not true.

For several days Joseph thought about what had happened. The uncertainty of mind he had felt changed to peace, love, and joy. He wanted to talk to someone who would appreciate his experience. One day while he was out, he saw a preacher who had been very friendly to him. He was sure the preacher could offer him some good advice.

"Is something on your mind, Joseph?" the preacher asked. "You seem about to burst."

Joseph nodded. "I have something to tell." Speaking softly, he told of his vision in the grove.

After the preacher heard the story, he said, "Joseph, my boy, you know as well as I do that there are no visions and revelations anymore. Such things ended with the Bible prophets." He leaned toward Joseph, looking into his eyes. "What you have experienced is straight from the devil. The sooner you forget about it, the better."

Joseph hurried away. He knew what he had seen, and he knew it had not come from the devil. Far from it. He could not deny the truth.

Before long, word of what he'd told the preacher got around. People didn't believe what had happened to him. They laughed and turned against him. Even his friends made fun of him. "Here comes Joe Smith," they said. "He sees things no one else does." They began calling him "Holy Joe."

The neighbors, who had been friendly before, gossiped about him. They teased him about "getting religion." Some people called him crazy. Terrible lies were told about him and his whole family.

Despite these problems, the Smiths went on working steadily to buy the land they had been farming. They agreed to pay $100 a year over several years for the land. The next year, on July 18, 1821, Mother Lucy gave birth to a daughter, Lucy, who would be her last baby. There were now nine children living in the log home, as well as the parents.

Alvin, who hired himself out wherever he could find work, began talking about building a new house. He offered to do most of the labor himself. "I want to have a nice, pleasant place for Father and Mother to sit in," he told the others,

People laughed and turned against Joseph.

"with everything arranged for their comfort. They shall not work anymore as they have done." Late in the year 1822, he started working on the house.

Although some people continued to persecute the family because of Joseph's claims, neighbors came to help them raise the house when it was time. By November of 1823 the frame was up, and the family arranged to get the rest of the materials they needed to finish it. They couldn't move into it yet because the house was just a skeleton without walls and a roof. But Alvin was determined to complete it.

During this time Joseph continued to think about the vision he'd had. As instructed, he did not join any of the churches in Palmyra. But sometimes he wondered if there was something else he should be doing.

At times, he wasn't as serious as he should have been, and he felt bad for the things he did wrong. He wanted to be forgiven for his boyish mistakes, and he wanted to find out more about what was expected of him.

On the night of September 21, 1823, when he was seventeen, he continued to pray long after others in the house had gone to sleep. As he knelt praying beside his sleeping brothers, he noticed a light. It was dim at first but got brighter until the room was lighter than at noonday. Suddenly an angel appeared, standing in the air. He wore a pure white robe, whiter than anything Joseph had ever seen.

Joseph continued to pray long after others in the house had gone to sleep.

When Joseph first saw the angel, he was frightened. But then his fear went away, and he felt calm as he listened. The visitor introduced himself as Moroni, a messenger sent from God. He said the Lord had important work for Joseph to do. Moroni told Joseph that his name would someday be known all over the world, and that people would say both good and evil things about him.

Moroni spoke of a book written on plates of gold. It told about people who lived in ancient America and how they came from Bible lands. Moroni and his ancestors were some of these people. The book contained the fulness of the everlasting gospel as delivered by Jesus himself to these people.

The book was hidden, Moroni explained, with two stones in silver frames called the Urim and Thummim. They were for translating the writing on the plates.

Moroni said that the book and the Urim and Thummim would be given to Joseph at a future date. "But," he said, "you must go soon to the hill where they are hidden and find them. You are not to tell anybody about them or show them unless God commands you to do so." If he disobeyed, the angel said, he would be destroyed.

While Moroni spoke about the plates of gold, Joseph saw a vision of the place where they were hidden, buried in a hill not far from the Smith farm.

As soon as Moroni finished speaking, the light in the room gathered around him. A shaft of light opened heavenward, and the angel rose up through it until he completely disappeared. The room was as dark as it had been before his appearance. Joseph lay exhausted.

As he pondered what the angel had told him, he noticed the room getting lighter again, and Moroni reappeared at his bedside.

The angel repeated the things he had said the first time. He also spoke of disasters that would come upon the earth, then went up in the pillar of light as before.

Joseph was wide awake now. To his surprise, Moroni appeared a third time, telling the same things yet again. He also cautioned Joseph, "Satan will try to tempt you, because your family is poor, to get the plates for the purpose of getting rich. This I forbid you."

Moroni said Joseph should have no other object in obtaining the plates but to glorify God and build His kingdom. "Otherwise," the angel warned, "you cannot get them." Before Moroni left, he also commanded, "You must tell your father what you have seen and heard tonight."

As the angel Moroni ascended the shaft of light for the third time, Joseph heard a rooster crow. It was morning. His visions of the angel had taken the whole night. His brothers were getting up, so Joseph did too.

He didn't feel it was the right time to tell of the night's events. Leaving the house, he went with his father and Alvin to a nearby field to continue harvesting. But as he worked with a sickle to cut the crop, his mind was filled with what the angel had said. Soon he stopped working to think about it.

Alvin came over to chide him. "If we don't keep working, we won't finish this field today, Joseph," he said.

Joseph began working again. But after a short time he felt so tired that he had to stop.

His father came striding over. Joseph knew he was coming to tell him to get back to work. But as his father gazed at his face he said, "Joseph, you look pale. Do you feel ill?"

Joseph nodded. "I have but little strength," he said.

His father examined him closely, then said, "Go back to the house and let your mother take care of you."

Joseph turned toward his home and began walking unsteadily. As he was climbing a fence between the field and the apple orchard, he fell unconscious on the grass under a tree.

When he finally woke up, he heard a voice calling him by name. Looking up, he saw Moroni for the fourth time. "Why did you not tell your father what I commanded you to tell him?" The angel's voice was stern.

"I was afraid my father would not believe me," Joseph whispered.

"He will believe every word you say to him," Moroni said. Then he repeated once again everything he had said during the night. "Now go to your father," he said, "and tell him."

Joseph promised to do so, and the angel left.

When he could walk, Joseph returned to the field. Alvin was still working, but their father was not there.

"Joseph," Alvin exclaimed, "why are you here? Father told you to go back to the house."

"I need to talk to him," Joseph said urgently. "Where is he?"

Alvin gestured toward the house. "Father went in. He was not feeling well."

Still weak, Joseph said, "Alvin, would you go tell him to come back here? I have something I must tell him."

Without asking questions, Alvin hurried away. Joseph sat down to wait and gather his strength.

When his father came, Joseph told him about Moroni's visits.

"My boy," his father said, "I want you to know that the angel was indeed a messenger from God. You must do as he told you to do."

Joseph thought about it. The first thing Moroni had told him to do was visit the nearby hill and find the hiding place of the golden plates. But what would come after that? The angel had spoken of his name becoming known throughout the world, for both good and evil.

Joseph was excited but anxious, wondering just exactly what lay ahead for him.

CHAPTER 5

THE STONE BOX

In the vision he'd had during the night, Joseph had seen where the golden plates were buried. They were in a thinly wooded section of a large nearby mound, the highest hill in the neighborhood. It was a mound that Joseph would learn to call the Hill Cumorah.

After Joseph's father told him to do what the angel had said, Joseph decided to go directly to the hill from the field where they'd been harvesting. As he hurried toward it, his mind raced excitedly.

"The plates contain a sacred record," he thought. "The fulness of the gospel. Nothing could be more important."

"Yes," came another thought. "And the plates are made of gold. Do you realize how much an ancient gold book would be worth?"

"But the book's message is worth more. That's what you should think about," he told himself.

"Yes, but think of all the good you could do with the money. You could help your parents pay for the farm and finish the house. Your family wouldn't have to work so hard, and you could help your friends, too."

With these thoughts going back and forth, he soon found himself at the hill.

When he got there, he climbed to the top and looked around, searching for the small grove of trees he'd seen in the vision. Before long he located it, close to where he was. Swiftly he walked to the grove.

Right away he saw what appeared to be a large, rounded rock, exactly as he'd seen in the vision. Falling to his knees, he scraped away the dirt and grass and found that the rock thinned down on either side so that it had the appearance of a curved lid. He tried to lift it, but it was too heavy. Leaping to his feet, he searched for a fallen branch thick enough to pry it up. When he found what he needed, he took it back to the rock, wedging one end under an edge.

Putting his full weight on the other end of the limb, he strained to lift the rock. He was sweating by the time he felt it shift a little. After digging away more of the dirt with his hands, he tried again to pry up the rock. His heart pounded when it slid aside and he saw that the lid covered a box made of stones held together with something like cement.

Falling again to his knees, he peered cautiously inside, catching his breath as he saw the dim glow of gold. The thin golden plates were there, bound together with three large rings, like a book. Thoughts of wealth again poured into his head. "There might be other things in the box worth just as much," said a tempting voice in his mind. "If you could just get those things, too . . ."

He reached into the hole to touch the plates and felt a physical shock shake his body. He tried twice more to take hold of them and twice more felt a shock. He'd been told to come here to find the golden plates. "Why can't I obtain the book?" he exclaimed aloud.

"Because you haven't kept the commandments of the Lord," came a voice. Unlike the tempting voice in his mind, this one came out loud from someone standing nearby.

Looking up, Joseph saw the Angel Moroni. Suddenly, he remembered all that Moroni had told him about Satan tempting him to use the plates to get rich. He felt awful and compared that cold feeling to the warmth he had felt during the night when Moroni first appeared and told him about the book. Wanting that warm feeling again, he began to pray. As he did so, his soul was

filled with the Spirit of the Lord. The heavens opened to him, and the glory of the Lord rested on him. He gazed with wonder at the scene.

"Look!" commanded the angel. Joseph looked and saw Satan surrounded by hosts of evil spirits.

Moroni spoke again. "All this is shown you, the good and the evil, that you may know the two powers and not be overcome by the wicked one. You now see why you could not obtain the plates. They are sacred and not for worldly glory. Their value is in the knowledge they give of the fulness of the gospel."

Moroni told Joseph he could not take the plates at that time but should return on the same day next year. He gave Joseph instructions to help strengthen him for what lay ahead. Humbled, Joseph left the hill and returned home, tears streaming down his face.

"Did you get the plates?" his father asked as soon as he stepped in the house.

"No, Father," Joseph replied, "I couldn't get them."

"Did you see them?"

"Yes. I saw them but could not take them."

Aloud, his Father wondered why.

"I could not get them," Joseph said, "for the angel of the Lord would not let me."

That evening his entire family gathered together, right down to little Lucy, who was now two years old. When they were all seated, with Lucy on the lap of Alvin, her favorite brother, Joseph told them of his experiences. He had more to say, but he felt so tired he could barely stay on his chair. Many things had happened that day, and he hadn't slept at all the night before because of the visits by the angel.

Seeing how exhausted Joseph looked, Alvin said, "Now, brother, let us go to bed and rise early in the morning in order to finish our day's work at an hour before sunset. Then, if Mother will get our supper early, we will all sit down for the purpose of listening to you while you tell us the great things which God has revealed to you."

Joseph agreed, happy to go to bed and get some rest.

The next evening, with his family together again, Joseph asked everyone to promise not to tell other people yet about his experiences. "The world is so wicked," he said, "that when people come to a knowledge of these things, some will try to take our lives. I must ask you to promise that you'll keep them secret until the time is right to reveal them."

After everyone agreed, Joseph continued telling them about his visions and the things he had learned. He told about the golden plates buried in the Hill Cumorah and about the instructions from the angel.

He never quite got over his astonishment that he, still a boy, had been chosen to eventually receive the plates. He had not as yet read the Bible all the way through. He felt that his older brothers, Alvin and Hyrum, were far better prepared to carry out the task placed on his shoulders. But he was willing to do his best.

On many evenings in the coming weeks the family sat amazed as Joseph talked about his experiences. Even though he hadn't been allowed to take the golden plates yet, he had learned from his heavenly visitor about the people described on them. He told his family about the ancient peoples of the Americas. He described their dress, the way they traveled, and the animals they rode. He related what the angel had told him about their buildings, the way they fought, and how they worshiped.

This was a happy time for the Smiths, and it drew them very close. They felt peaceful, knowing that God was about to reveal something that would help them understand His eternal plan for the happiness and salvation of all people.

But on November 15, 1823, tragedy struck the family. About ten o'clock in the morning, Alvin was taken very ill with terrible pains in his abdomen. He came in from the field where he'd been working. "Father," he said, "would you go immediately for a doctor?"

His father hurried away, returning soon with a Dr. Greenwood, since Dr. McIntyre, their regular doctor, was away for a few days.

Dr. Greenwood offered Alvin a large dose of medicine. At first Alvin refused to take it. But his pain was so intense that he finally agreed to do so. It lodged in his stomach, and all the medicines given him later failed to move it. On the third day of Alvin's illness, Dr. McIntyre returned home and came to see him, bringing four other doctors with him. They examined Alvin, but nothing they did made him feel any better.

"I am going to die," Alvin said.

"No, Alvin," Joseph cried. "We can't get along without you. Do not speak of dying."

Alvin reached for Joseph's hand. "I feel so terrible that I know my time is very short."

He then asked that his brothers and sisters be brought to his side so he could give them some parting advice. He asked Hyrum to take over the building of the new house. "See that it is finished so that our dear parents can be more comfortable in their old age," he said.

He told Sophronia to help take care of their parents too.

To Joseph he said, "Be a good boy and do everything in your power to bring to pass the things that have been promised to you." He gripped Joseph's hand. "Be faithful in receiving instruction and in keeping every commandment that is given you. Your brother Alvin must leave you; but remember the example which he has set for you."

Tearfully, Joseph said he would do what Alvin asked.

After all the other children had been in to see him, Alvin requested that little Lucy be brought.

His mother went to wake the baby, whose eyes grew large when she was told that her beloved Amby, her own name for him, wanted to see her. Mother Lucy carried her to Alvin's bed. The little girl sprang from her mother's arms and caught him around the neck. "Oh, Amby, Amby," she cried, kissing him again and again.

"Lucy," Alvin said, "you must be the best girl in the world, and take care of Mother. You can't have your Amby anymore. Amby is going away. He must leave little Lucy."

He then kissed her good-bye and asked his family to take her away despite her pleas to stay. Moments later on that 19th day of November, 1823, Alvin died. He was twenty-five years old.

Little Lucy cried to go back to him, but Sophronia held her in her arms and would not let her loose. "Lucy," Sophronia said, "your Amby is gone now. An angel has taken his spirit to heaven."

Joseph felt that his heart would break. He could not think of going on without Alvin. He could not face the empty chair now when the family gathered each evening. He gave up repeating the stories the angel had told him. Instead, when the family gathered together, they sat and wept over their loss.

CHAPTER 6

GOOD NEWS AND BAD

After Alvin's death, Joseph and Hyrum did their best to keep the promises they'd made to him. One thing they needed to do was to help finish the house for their parents.

The family hired a neighbor with house-building skills to do some of the work. The Smiths helped paint and prepare the house to move in. When they finished, they had a wonderful farm home with a central chimney, white walls inside, and red woodwork. With five rooms on the main floor and a big, unfinished room upstairs, it gave the Smiths much more space in which to live with their large family.

Together with the barn, a cooper's shop, and other outdoor buildings, and the fields, garden, and orchard, it made a handsome sight. The house would give Mother Lucy and Father Joseph the comfort Alvin had dreamed of.

The place was so nice that the man who helped the Smiths build the house offered them $1,500 for the whole farm. That was a lot of money, but they weren't tempted to sell it, even though they still owed the man some money. They'd worked too hard for the house and looked forward to enjoying it for many years. If they just kept working hard, they would soon be able to finish paying for it all.

Shortly before the house was finished, Joseph got a chance to earn some of the money the family needed. In the fall of 1825, a man named Josiah Stowell from Pennsylvania came to Palmyra looking for Joseph, who was now almost twenty. Mr. Stowell had heard stories that Joseph could find treasure buried in the earth. He hoped Joseph would use his unusual power to help find a silver mine.

Joseph wasn't comfortable with Mr. Stowell's proposal.

"Listen to me," Josiah Stowell said. He then told Joseph a story about a group of Spaniards who many years before had a silver mine near Harmony, Pennsylvania. "When it came time to leave, they buried some of the silver in a cave by the river. They never came back to get it. With your help, I think we may be able to find it."

"How do you know the story is true?" Joseph asked.

Mr. Stowell shrugged. "I have no proof. But think how wonderful it would be if it did turn out to be true. If you help me out, we can find out for sure."

"No." Joseph shook his head. "Can't you find someone where you live to do the digging?"

"I want you to do it," Josiah Stowell said. He offered Joseph money to dig for him, whether they found the mine or not.

Joseph thought how badly his family needed money and finally agreed to do what Mr. Stowell asked. He went with Mr. Stowell to Harmony, Pennsylvania, and helped him dig.

They continued the work for nearly a month without success. Joseph told Mr. Stowell that it was no use to continue. Reluctantly Mr. Stowell agreed that they should stop digging.

Joseph did not find the Spanish treasure, but he did find a treasure of quite a different kind. While in Harmony, he boarded with a family by the name of Hale. They had a daughter named Emma, a pretty girl with dark hair and hazel eyes. Joseph enjoyed her good humor and bright personality. He liked the way she cheerfully went about her work. He spent as much time as he could with her.

But not long after he gave up digging for Mr. Stowell, Joseph decided to return to his family in New York. Though he hadn't known Emma long, he liked her a lot and would think about her often while they were apart.

When Joseph got home, he learned that a new land agent had been assigned to the area that included the farm his family was buying. They still owed one payment on it and weren't quite sure where they would get the money.

It was a difficult time for the Smith family. But one thing gave them hope. Mr. Stowell came back to Palmyra with his friend, Joseph Knight, looking for wheat or flour to buy. Since the Smiths had planted wheat and expected a good crop, they made a contract with the two men. They agreed to deliver to the men a certain amount of wheat. In return, they would receive enough money to make the final payment on the farm.

Hyrum told the land agent they would have the money around Christmas time.

After the harvest, the wheat was delivered to Mr. Stowell and Mr. Knight. In December Father Joseph prepared to go to Pennsylvania to get the money for it. Joseph had been thinking a lot about the lovely girl he had met in Harmony. When his father was ready to go, Joseph pulled his parents aside and said, "I would like to go with you, Father. I've been lonely since Alvin died, and if you have no objection, I would like to get married to Miss Emma Hale, if she will have me."

His parents smiled at his eagerness and looked at each other understandingly. "We have no objection," Father Joseph said. "In fact, we hope you'll bring her home with you so we may enjoy her company."

Joseph and his father set out for Pennsylvania with everything looking bright and hopeful for their family. For the first time since Joseph had been born, they would own a farm and a comfortable home. Life seemed good.

It seemed even better when they got to the Hale house. Emma was excited to see Joseph again. He could tell that she liked him as much as he liked her.

But Emma's parents were not as pleased to see Joseph as Emma was. They wanted their daughter to marry well, and to them, Joseph was just a boy who had helped Josiah Stowell dig for treasure.

"They'll accept you eventually," Emma assured Joseph.

Meanwhile, Joseph's father, as he was returning to Palmyra, received an urgent letter from Hyrum. "Hurry home," Hyrum had written. "We're about to lose everything."

He hurried home to bad news. The man who had helped to build their house had nearly succeeded in taking it away from them. He and his friends had told the land agent that Joseph and his father had left town to avoid making the last payment and that Hyrum was wrecking the farm.

Believing their lies, the agent sold the land to the man, giving him the deed.

By the time the truth came out, it was too late for the Smiths to save the farm. But they were able to make the thieves sell the place to a more friendly man, who let the Smiths rent it.

That was better than being kicked off the farm completely. But still it was a sad time for the family. Just a short time before, life was going well, and their dreams of owning a farm and home were about to come true. Now suddenly they were back where they had begun.

Joseph spent most of the next few months working in southern New York, not too far from Harmony, Pennsylvania. He went to Harmony whenever possible to visit Emma.

But Emma's father, Isaac Hale, still did not like him. He looked down on Joseph and thought he was rough and careless, especially compared with Emma, who was a schoolteacher. Isaac Hale refused to let his daughter marry Joseph.

Over the next while, Joseph tried to better himself. He went to school. Friends who knew of his honesty and hard work helped him out. Martin Harris, a Palmyra farmer Joseph had worked for, bought him a new suit of clothes. Mr. Knight, who thought Joseph was the best worker he'd ever hired, let him use his horse and sleigh to visit Emma.

Emma made it plain that she liked this handsome young man who appeared so often at her door. At age twenty, Joseph was six feet tall and muscular, like his father. He had blue eyes under thick eyelashes, and light auburn hair. His smile was easy and warm.

When Emma asked her father once again to approve her marriage to Joseph, he once again bellowed his refusal.

Discouraged, Joseph returned to Palmyra, arriving in time for his yearly visit to the Hill Cumorah, on September 22, 1826. But it wasn't long before he headed back to Harmony. Hyrum had recently married, and that only made Joseph lonelier for Emma. He was determined to do something about his love for her.

Mr. Stowell showed him what he could do. "You're twenty-one years old now," he said, "and Emma is twenty-two. You're legally old enough to make your own decisions. You don't need Mr. Hale's permission to get married." Emma soon agreed, and on January 18, 1827, they quickly and quietly got married. Nobody from either of their families was present.

After their marriage, Emma went back to Palmyra with Joseph. They settled down to live with the Smiths, and Joseph again became part of the family farming operation. Now happily married, Joseph and Emma looked forward to what the future might hold.

Chapter 7

Joseph Receives the Golden Plates

Knowing that he was soon to return to the place where the golden plates were buried for his next appointment with the angel, Joseph continued preparing himself to be worthy. He felt he would get the plates this year, but he worried about what would happen then. Tales of how he had found a "gold bible" had gotten out, and he was afraid people would try to steal the plates from him.

He and Emma talked about it. "I'll need to go to the hill after midnight during the early hours of September 22," Joseph explained. "Fortunately, most people will be asleep then."

Emma nodded. "I'll go with you and keep watch while you speak with the angel."

"Thank you, Emma," Joseph said. "Are you sure you won't be afraid?"

"Not if you're there," Emma told him. Joseph smiled at his bride.

They still had a few details to work out, such as how they would get there and back and where they would put the plates once they brought them home.

Joseph's mother stayed up late working on the night of September 21. Around midnight, Joseph asked her for a chest with a lock and key. The family had chests, but his mother said none of the locks were working. She grew worried, afraid that not having a locking chest might keep Joseph from getting the plates. "Never mind," Joseph said, calming her. "I can do very well just now without it."

Soon Emma came in wearing her riding dress and bonnet, and she and Joseph left the house. Mr. Knight and Mr. Stowell had stopped by to stay with the Smiths for a couple of days. Joseph and Emma quietly borrowed Mr. Knight's horse and wagon and headed to the hill.

Joseph guided the horse as Emma held the lantern. They proceeded slowly so that the wagon would not rattle too much and wake people along the way. It was almost pitch black outside, with only the faintest sliver of a moon. Occasional clouds scudded across it, blocking out what little light it provided.

At the bottom of the hill, Joseph stopped the wagon. "All right, Emma," he whispered. "I'll be back soon."

He asked if she wanted him to leave the lantern. "No," she said. "I'll be less likely to be seen here in the darkness."

Grasping the handle of the lantern, Joseph climbed the hill to the clearing where the stone box was buried. He was puffing by the time he reached it, partly from the exertion and partly from nervousness. The angel had told him, he remembered, that if he accepted the call to translate the plates, he would be severely persecuted. His life would never again be the same. As the angel had said, his name would someday be known for both good and evil throughout the world.

He wondered if he could do it. But there was no turning back now.

As Joseph cleared the dirt and grass away from the stone lid, the Angel Moroni once again appeared, lighting up the clearing. "You have been found worthy, Joseph," he said.

This time, as Joseph lifted the ancient record from its hiding place, he could see it clearly in the glow from the angel. He had seen it before, of course, but this time it was his to study and translate.

The record was engraved on plates that looked like gold. Each plate was about seven by eight inches in width and length, and not quite as thick as

Satisfied that they were safe, Joseph returned to where Emma waited with the horse and wagon.

common tin. Both sides were covered with engravings of ancient characters. All together, the plates were about six inches thick. The three rings running through the plates at one edge bound them together like a book.

As he gazed at the plates, Joseph heard Moroni tell him that he would now be responsible for them. "You must use every effort to preserve them," the angel said, "until I return to take them back."

Then Moroni disappeared, and the clearing was dark except for the dim flicker of the lantern.

Quickly Joseph reached back down into the box to get the interpreters, the Urim and Thummim, which resembled eyeglasses. He stood up. The golden plates were heavy. Over fifty pounds, Joseph guessed.

His heart thumped. Now that he had them, what should he do with them? If he took them back to the house, the family and Mr. Knight would surely want to see them. The angel had warned him several times that he must not show them to anyone.

Joseph quickly took off his coat to wrap around the plates and the Urim and Thummim. He felt he had to shield them from curious eyes, even though no one else was there. Starting down the hill, he hoped the light from the lantern and the pale glimmer from the moon would show him a place where he could hide the plates for a few hours. He needed time to plan how to carry out the huge job he'd been given.

In the dark woods on the hillside, Joseph found a fallen log with a hollow large enough to hide the plates. After covering them with dead leaves and twigs, he held up the lantern to make sure nothing could be seen of them. Satisfied that they were safe, he returned to where Emma waited with the horse and wagon.

CHAPTER 8

HIDING THE PLATES

Joseph handed the lantern to Emma as he climbed into the wagon and got settled.

"Did you get the plates?" Emma whispered.

"Yes," Joseph said. He told her about leaving them in the hollow log. "I must have someone make me a strong chest to put them in before I take them home," he said.

He urged the horse forward, and soon they were back at the Smith farm. Although it was barely dawn, they found that Joseph's family and Mr. Knight were already up. During breakfast, Joseph didn't say a word about getting the plates.

After breakfast, however, Joseph called Mr. Knight into another room. He had earlier told him about his hopes of obtaining the plates, and Mr. Knight was anxious to hear what had happened.

Joseph put his foot up on a bed and leaned his head on his hand. Looking serious, he said, "Well, I am disappointed."

"I'm sorry," replied Mr. Knight sadly.

"I am greatly disappointed," Joseph continued, shaking his head. Then breaking into a broad smile, he exclaimed, "It is ten times better than I expected." He went on to describe the plates to Mr. Knight in detail. "They are written in characters," Joseph said, "I want them translated."

Joseph didn't tell very many people about the plates. But he knew it would be impossible to keep the matter secret for very long.

The next day, September 23, he got up very early to go to a nearby village to repair a well. He hoped to earn enough money to pay a cabinetmaker to build a sturdy chest in which to keep the plates.

Soon after he left, a neighbor came to the farm and began asking Joseph's father about the treasure Joseph had found. His father was alarmed that the word had already gotten out. He refused to answer the man's questions, but he learned that ten or twelve men had joined together to look for the treasure. They had hired a conjuror, a person who deals with magic, to find the hiding place.

Determined to learn all he could about this gang, Father Joseph strolled through the neighborhood. At the first house he came to, he found the conjuror with a group of men outside in the yard.

Greeting the men pleasantly, Father Joseph knocked at the door, asking the lady of the house if he could please take a look at their newspaper. He left the door slightly open, and when the lady offered him a chair, he put it where he could hear the talking going on outside.

"What we want to do is find Joe Smith's gold bible," one of the men told the conjuror. "Must be worth a lot of money."

"Tell me about it," the conjuror said, sounding very interested.

The lady of the house, apparently realizing that Father Joseph was listening to their plans, slipped outside. Through the partly open door, Father Joseph saw her whisper to her husband and gesture toward him, putting a hand up to her ear. He knew she was telling the men that he was listening and that they should not talk so loud.

"I don't care who's listening," the conjuror yelled. "We will have the plates in spite of Joe Smith or the devil." All of the men laughed and jeered.

When the lady crept back into the house, Father Joseph casually laid down the newspaper. "I don't have time to finish reading it right now," he remarked. After thanking her politely, he left.

Hurrying home, he asked Emma if she knew where the plates were.

"No," she said. "Joseph left them hidden somewhere on the hill."

Father Joseph told her about the plot to find them. "I hope Joseph hasn't made a mistake leaving them there," he said.

"If I had a horse," Emma said, "I would go see him. He should know what's going on."

"You shall have one in fifteen minutes," Father Joseph said. "I'll have William bring it."

When William came with the horse, Emma got on immediately and rode off to where Joseph was working. There she found that he had already come up out of the well he'd been repairing.

"I've had a very uneasy feeling about the plates," he said.

Quickly she informed him about the plot that was developing with the mob and the conjuror.

"The plates are well hidden," Joseph said. "But I think I should return home with you in case something happens."

Without removing the rough linen coat he'd put on to cover his clothes while he dug, Joseph leaped onto his horse, and he and Emma rode off.

At home they found Father Joseph pacing anxiously in the yard.

"Father," Joseph said, "there is no danger. All is perfectly safe. There is no cause for alarm."

"How can you be sure?" his father asked.

Joseph didn't answer his question. Instead he wiped his forehead with a handkerchief and said wearily, "I've spent the whole day hard at work. I need something to eat and drink."

While he ate, Joseph sent his youngest brother, Don Carlos, to Hyrum's house nearby. "Tell him I need to talk to him right away," he instructed Don Carlos. He knew that Hyrum's wife, Jerusha, was in bed with their first baby and that Hyrum wouldn't want to leave her. So he told Don Carlos, "Tell him it's very important, but that I won't keep him for very long."

Don Carlos ran off to convey the message, and Hyrum came immediately.

"I'm going to bring the plates home today," Joseph told him, "and I need a safe place to keep them. Do you have a strong chest with a lock and key that I can use?"

Hyrum nodded. "I'll go get it right now." He hastened back to his home.

When he had finished eating, Joseph went alone to the Hill Cumorah to get the golden plates. Traveling a back route through groves of trees, he hoped no one would see him and follow.

He found the fallen log where he'd hidden the golden plates and quickly pulled out the leaves and bark he'd used to conceal them. He was very relieved to see that the plates were still safe.

Removing the coat that still covered his clothes, he lifted the plates from the hole and wrapped them in it. Awkwardly carrying the heavy bundle under his arm, he started home, walking through the woods. The autumn leaves crunched under his feet, and he worried that they were too noisy.

Suddenly, as he climbed over a fallen tree, a man rose up from behind it and struck him with the butt of a gun. Though severely bruised, Joseph was able to turn and knock the man down with his free hand, holding the heavy bundle with the plates tightly under his other arm. He then ran on as fast as he could.

Half a mile farther on, he was attacked again and fought off the second attacker just as he had the first. Before he reached the house, he was assaulted once more. When he struck this attacker, he dislocated his own thumb. He hardly noticed as he dashed on.

By the time Joseph got near home, he was so tired he plopped down by the fence to rest. When he'd caught his breath, he raced to the house and through the door with the plates still wrapped in his coat.

His sixteen-year-old brother William saw the coat and knew immediately what was wrapped inside of it. "What, Joseph?" the boy asked in disbelief. "Can't we see them?"

"No," Joseph answered breathlessly. "I was disobedient the first time, but I intend to be faithful this time. The angel commanded me not to show them until they are translated."

Worn out from his ordeal, Joseph fell against a wall, panting. When he'd rested for a moment, he asked, "Has Hyrum brought the chest?"

"No," his mother said.

"Please, Mother," Joseph said. "Send Don Carlos out to find Father and Mr. Knight and Mr. Stowell. I want them to find the men who attacked me."

Joseph rested while Don Carlos hurried off on his errand. The boy returned soon, reporting that the three men had gone to search for the attackers. "Now, little brother," Joseph said, "go to Hyrum's house and tell him to bring over the chest I asked him for. Tell him to hurry. I thought he would be here already."

Again Don Carlos hurried away. It wasn't long before he returned with Hyrum, who carried a chest on his shoulder. "I'm sorry I wasn't here earlier," he apologized. "But I stopped to sit a while with Jerusha and our baby."

"It's all right," Joseph said. "Go back now and be with your wife."

Hyrum left, and Joseph swiftly put the plates inside the chest, which he locked. Then he lay down to rest and nurse his painful thumb.

By the time he felt able to get up, Father Joseph, Mr. Knight, and Mr. Stowell had returned. They were talking in the kitchen with some friends. They said they hadn't found the attackers.

Although he joined in the conversation, Joseph stopped soon and held up his throbbing thumb. "I must stop talking, Father," he said, "and get you to put my thumb in place, for it is very painful." Taking a deep breath, he held it out to his father, who quickly wrenched it back into place. Feeling somewhat better, Joseph was able to go on talking with the friends.

For the next few days Joseph worked on their farm. He wanted to stay as close as possible in case there was trouble. One afternoon, feeling uneasy, he ran into the house and asked his mother if she had seen anybody skulking in the area.

"Not a single soul," she said. "I have seen no one since you left for the fields this morning."

Joseph peered out of a window. "I thought I saw shadowy forms about," he said. "I have a feeling that a mob will come tonight to search for the plates." Earlier, Joseph had taken the plates from the chest, wrapped them in a linen cloth, and put them in a small box. "We must hide them," he said. "But where?"

Mother Lucy looked around too. "Under the fireplace hearth," she suggested. "They'll not find them there."

They scurried to take up the bricks, burying the box in the dirt underneath, then re-laying the bricks so nobody could tell anything had been disturbed.

Don Carlos was sent to bring Father Joseph, Hyrum, Samuel, and William in from the fields. They had no sooner gotten there than an armed mob marched into the yard. The Smiths were far outnumbered.

Joseph recalled a story his grandfather Solomon Mack had told him. During his days as a soldier, Grandfather Mack had once found himself outnumbered in a dangerous situation. His enemies were coming toward him, weapons raised. Alone except for a friend who was behind him in the woods, he knew he was in danger. "There was no way to escape," his Grandfather Mack had told Joseph, "unless I could do it by stratagem. So I rushed upon them, calling in the meantime at the top of my voice, 'Rush on! Rush on, my boys.'"

The only weapon he'd had was a walking staff. He had held it high as he'd charged toward the enemies. At the same time his friend had dashed out of the trees. The enemies, thinking there was a large group of men behind them, turned and ran away.

Remembering this story, Joseph threw open the door, yelling as if he had an army behind him. All of the men of the family, from Father Joseph down to young Don Carlos, ran out of the house with such fury that the mob, looking totally dismayed, fled into the woods and disappeared.

Joseph knew that other mobs would come, seeking to take the plates for their own gain. He dug the box from under the hearth, took out the plates, and wrapped them in layers of clothing. Carrying them across the road to his father's cooper's shop, he concealed them in the loft.

Other mobbers did come but were never able to find the plates.

CHAPTER 9

TROUBLE WITH LUCY HARRIS

Joseph was eager to start translating the golden plates. He knew it wasn't going to be easy, with so many people wanting to get a look at them. There was also the danger that someone would try to steal them, and Joseph had promised the Angel Moroni that he would keep them safe.

He decided he needed help. Martin Harris was a good man and a wise family friend who had told Joseph he would help him in any way he could. One day Joseph asked his mother to take a message to Mr. Harris.

His mother seemed reluctant. She was making bread, and she took time to add more flour before she answered. "Joseph," she said finally, "this is something I really do not want to do."

Joseph was perplexed. "But why, Mother? It's a simple enough task."

His mother folded over the bread dough, pounded it, and folded it again before she said, "It's his wife I don't want to see. You know what a . . ." She hesitated, seeming to hunt for the right word. "You know what a peculiar woman Lucy Harris is. She'll demand to know why I want to see Martin. And she'll be jealous that you want to talk to him and not her."

Joseph grinned. He knew all about Lucy Harris. "Well, Mother," he said, "she's quite hard of hearing. Can't you tell Martin quietly so that she doesn't know what you're saying?"

His mother stopped mixing the bread to look at him. "You know what happens when she doesn't hear something that's said. She suspects that it's being kept a secret from her. That makes her even more difficult to deal with." She shook her head. "I'd rather not go to the Harris home."

"Mother," Joseph said, "this is very important. I can't go myself because there are many eyes watching everything I do. Father and Hyrum and the other boys are away at work. Emma does not know the Harrises well. I can't send one of the younger children because they wouldn't know how to handle Lucy the way you do."

His mother pulled off a hunk of dough and worked it into a loaf shape. "All right, son. But I know I'll have to tell her something about what's been happening before she'll let me speak to Martin."

Now it was Joseph's turn to hesitate. "Well," he said, "she's probably heard all kinds of rumors already. So you may tell her the truth of the matter."

"As soon as I finish the bread," his mother agreed, "I'll go see her."

"Thank you, Mother," Joseph said gently.

When Joseph's mother arrived at the Harris home, Lucy Harris welcomed her inside. "I'm happy to see you, Mrs. Smith," she said. "My sister is visiting and we've been discussing your boy Joe and that gold bible he said he found. Come in and tell us about it."

Mother Lucy greeted both women and then sat down at Mrs. Harris's invitation. She began to explain her errand for Joseph, but Mrs. Harris interrupted. "He'll be translating that record soon, won't he? I've got some money I can give to help him get started."

Her sister leaned forward. "I'd like to give some too, Mrs. Smith. I can offer $75. That should help him out."

"No, no." Mother Lucy shook her head. "I don't want your money. I came on no such business."

Mrs. Harris went to a chest against the wall. After rummaging in it for a moment, she came back, holding out some money. "Here," she said to Mother Lucy, "I want you to take this $200 to Joseph."

Again Mother Lucy shook her head. "Thank you, but no." She wondered what the sisters had in mind. Did they think of the golden plates as "treasure"? Did they hope to get a share of it by offering money? Or did they somehow want to buy their way into Joseph's project?

Perhaps they were just being generous because they knew Joseph didn't have much money.

Whatever their reasons, Mother Lucy knew that she could not take the money. "I must let Joseph attend to things like that," she said.

She smiled at Mrs. Harris and her sister before saying, "What I came for was to speak with Mr. Harris. Then I must return home, as my family will be expecting me."

"I never heard of anybody refusing money when they need it so badly," Mrs. Harris complained grumpily.

When Mother Lucy shook her head yet again, Mrs. Harris took her to another room where her husband, Martin, was laying the last few bricks of a fireplace hearth.

Martin nodded when Mother Lucy explained that Joseph would like to see him. "I'll be at your house in a few days to talk to him," he said.

"And I am coming to see him too," Mrs. Harris declared. "I will be there on Tuesday afternoon and will stop overnight."

Not too happy about that prospect, Mother Lucy went home.

The next Tuesday, true to her word, Lucy Harris showed up at the Smith home. As soon as she was invited inside, she began to question Joseph. "Did you really find a golden book? Just exactly where did you find it? When will you show me the golden plates? I'm going to give you money to publish your translation. Doesn't that give me the right to see the plates?"

Joseph felt weighted down by her many questions. "I cannot show them to you, Mrs. Harris," he said firmly. "I thank you kindly for your concern, but I cannot accept your help at this time."

Mrs. Harris gazed skeptically at him. "Now, Joseph," she challenged, "are you not telling me a lie? Can you look full in my eye and say that you have in reality found a record, as you pretend?"

Joseph looked her full in the eye. "I can."

"All right," she said. "I will tell you what I'll do. If I can get a witness that you speak the truth, I'll believe all you say about the matter." She lifted her chin. "I mean to help you anyway."

She refused to accept Joseph's protests.

As she had previously stated, she stayed the night with the Smiths. But the next day she seemed a changed woman. Pulling Joseph aside in the busy morning household, she told him she'd had a dream.

"Or perhaps it was a vision, like you've had," she said. "A personage appeared to me and told me I asked too many improper questions of a servant of the Lord. After that, he held out something in his hands and said, 'Behold, here are the plates; look upon them, and believe.'"

She then went on to describe the golden plates in remarkable detail, right down to the strange engravings on them.

"Now I have seen them," she said, "if only in a dream. And I insist on giving you money to get started with the translation."

Joseph, deciding this was the only way he could end her coaxing, finally accepted the money. "As a loan," he told her. "I will pay you back when I can."

Satisfied with this, Lucy Harris turned to leave. "Now, you must not wait any longer to begin the translation," she instructed Joseph. "And I want to be kept informed about the progress you are making." Calling good-bye to Mother Lucy, she left.

Joseph felt uneasy, wondering if he might have further trouble with her. But she was right about one thing. He must get started with the translation.

CHAPTER 10

THE TRANSLATION BEGINS

As he had promised, Martin Harris came to the Smith home a few days later. Joseph told him about the difficulties he saw ahead as he started to translate the golden plates. "I'm constantly disturbed by people asking to see them," he said. "When I refuse to show them, they call me 'Holy Joe' and insist that I should share the treasure I found."

Joseph told Martin that people persecuted his family, too, jeering at them and saying nasty things.

There were also money worries. It would cost a lot to get the book printed, once the translating was finished. Joseph felt he should be working on the farm to feed his family as well as earn the money.

Martin nodded. "I understand," he said. "But despite the problems, you must get on with the translation work." He promised to contribute as much money as he could to help.

By this time Emma was expecting a baby and not feeling well. She yearned to be closer to her parents. They had not been very friendly since she had eloped with Joseph. But when she wrote to them about the coming baby, they wrote that they were delighted. They invited her and Joseph to come back to Harmony and live with them.

Both Emma and Joseph saw this as an answer to their prayers. Emma could have her baby in the midst of her family, and Joseph could take the plates to a new place where he could translate them in peace.

In December 1827, Emma's brother Alva came up from Pennsylvania with a wagon and team of horses to help them move. While Joseph and Alva were in town taking care of some business, Martin Harris walked up to Joseph and gave him a bag with fifty dollars in it to help out. Joseph thanked him for his kindness and offered to pay him back later when he could. Martin insisted he did not want it back.

"It's to help you do the Lord's work," Martin said. "I want you to leave Palmyra right away. There is a lot of excitement in the village. A number of men are threatening to form a mob to tar and feather you. It's unsafe for you to remain here."

"Thank you, Martin," Joseph said. "You are a good friend. The Lord will bless you for this kindness."

"You must leave in the dark of night," Martin said. "And cut some strong sticks to use as weapons in case a mob follows you."

Joseph agreed to do as he said.

With the help of his family and Alva, Joseph loaded his and Emma's belongings into a wagon. To protect the golden plates, he put them and the Urim and Thummim inside a wooden box, which he hid in a barrel of beans with a strong lid.

In the meantime Emma had heated some bricks in the fireplace to keep their feet warm. Soon they started off on their journey through the cold December night.

It took them several days to get to Harmony. When they finally arrived, Emma's family welcomed them joyfully. But immediately there was a problem. Emma's father, Isaac Hale, knew that Joseph now had the golden plates. He wanted to see them.

Joseph dug the wooden box out of the barrel of beans. "They are here, inside," he said.

"Open the box," Isaac insisted.

"I can't," Joseph said. "The angel told me I could not show the plates to anyone."

Isaac scowled. "I will not allow anything inside my house that I am not allowed to see."

"Very well," Joseph said. "I will take them elsewhere."

For a few days he hid the box containing the plates in the woods. He and Emma decided that he would not be able to begin the translation in the main house with the family. When they told Isaac, he said that despite his dislike for Joseph, he wanted to keep his daughter close by. "You may have the small house across the way," he said.

Gratefully, Joseph and Emma cleaned the little house and moved in their belongings.

When they were settled, Joseph took the box containing the golden plates to a small upstairs room where he could have privacy. Before long, however, he realized that with only Emma and himself in the house, he could do much of his translating downstairs on the main floor. At times, the plates were lying on a table wrapped in cloth, and Emma dusted around and even felt them through the cloth as she worked. But she never looked at them.

By now Isaac Hale had told several neighbors about Joseph's "treasure." They began coming to the house, curious to see it. Some even offered Joseph money to show them the plates. When he would not, they grumbled. But they did not make trouble the way the mobs in Palmyra had done.

Now at last Joseph could begin the work of translating the engravings on the golden plates. He knew nothing of the language in which they were written. But if he followed the instructions the Angel Moroni had given him, using the Urim and Thummim and concentrating very hard, the meaning of the characters came into his mind and he could write it down.

He wrote with a steel-tipped pen that had to be dipped in ink every few words. His paper was plain foolscap, called that because of the jester's cap watermark on it.

It was a slow and tedious process, and sometimes Joseph asked Emma to write out what he dictated from the plates. Both of them were excited as the story of an ancient people began to take shape.

Chapter 11

The 116 Pages

Back in Palmyra, Martin Harris decided that he should go visit Joseph. Before Joseph had ever left for Pennsylvania, the two of them had talked, and Martin had promised to visit after Joseph got settled. Now that some time had passed, Martin was anxious to see Joseph again.

When Martin told his wife, Lucy, what he planned to do, she insisted that she should go along with him. Martin didn't think this was a good idea. Early one morning he left the house secretly and headed for Pennsylvania.

Lucy Harris was furious when she discovered Martin was gone. Storming over to Joseph's parents' house, she demanded to know where Martin was.

"Why, Mrs. Harris, I thought you knew," Mother Lucy said. "He and Hyrum left to go see Joseph this morning. Before daylight."

Mrs. Harris's face reddened. "Why did you let them go without me?" she shouted.

Mother Lucy was baffled. "I had no idea you planned to go with them. Perhaps you can go another time."

Mrs. Harris refused to be soothed. "This isn't the end of it," she cried. "Mark my words. I will have satisfaction for the treatment I have received."

She stomped from the room, leaving Mother Lucy wondering what manner of trouble she might cause.

It took Martin and Hyrum several days to get to Harmony, Pennsylvania. As soon as they arrived at Joseph's home, Martin excitedly described what had happened to him.

"After I gave money to help you and Emma move to Pennsylvania," Martin explained, "I had a vision or dream. In it, the Lord showed me the marvelous work that He was about to do."

"That was a blessing from the Lord," Joseph confirmed, "for your faith and righteous works."

"In my dream," Martin continued eagerly, "the Lord showed me that I must go to New York City with some of the characters from the plates and show them to learned men to see if they can translate them."

"I've already copied a lot of characters from the plates," Joseph said, "and I've translated some of them. You should do as the Lord has directed and take a copy of some of the characters and the translation to New York."

In February 1828, Martin set out for New York City with the documents. He found his way to Professor Charles Anthon, a man known for his work in ancient languages. Martin later reported that Professor Anthon said the characters Joseph had copied were from the old Egyptian, Chaldaic, Assyriac, and Arabic languages. Martin said the professor gave him a certificate saying this and also that the translation was correct.

"Then when I was leaving," Martin told Joseph, "Professor Anthon called me back to ask how you found out there were golden plates in the Hill Cumorah. I said that an angel of God revealed it to you."

"What did he say about that?" Joseph asked.

Martin twisted his hands. "He asked me to give back the certificate he'd signed, and he tore it to pieces. He said there are no such things as angels. He said the only way he will verify the plates is if you will bring them to him."

Joseph shook his head. "I can't do that unless the angel tells me to."

"Yes, I know," Martin said. "But from what he said at first, I am convinced that what you say is true."

Joseph smiled. "I know that it is true without the word of an expert. I intend to go on translating as fast as I can." He stopped, frowning. "But I need a scribe. Emma helps me whenever she can, but she is very busy with the housework. And sometimes she doesn't feel well because of the coming baby."

"I will gladly serve as your scribe," Martin said. "Let me return home to settle my affairs. When I come back, I will do anything I can to help you."

When Martin arrived home in Palmyra, he found his wife, Lucy, very angry with him. To calm her down, he showed her the transcript of the ancient characters from the plates and the translation he had taken to Professor Anthon.

She examined it all with fascination. "May I keep this for a while?" she asked.

Not sure he could trust her, Martin said no. That made Lucy angrier than ever.

When Martin made preparations to go back to Pennsylvania to serve as Joseph's scribe, his wife insisted on going with him. "You're not going without me this time," she told him.

Martin had no choice. He loaded the wagon, and they set out on the long trip. When they arrived at Joseph and Emma's home, Lucy informed them that the reason she had come was to see the golden plates. "I will not leave until I've seen them," she said.

Joseph shook his head. "I'm sorry, Mrs. Harris. I can't let you see them."

Lucy was furious. She began ransacking the house. Martin, as well as Joseph and Emma, tried to stop her, but she was strong and very determined.

Joseph, seeing that she would not stop until she found the plates, slipped them out of the house to a hiding place.

When Lucy had finally rummaged in every trunk and cupboard and chest without success, she said, "Well, Joseph, I've concluded that you've buried them outdoors."

The next day she searched through the woods despite the cold winter weather. She found nothing. She came inside and told Emma she had been scared by a large black snake. Emma said there were no snakes in that area during the winter. Unable to find what she was looking for, Lucy packed up her things and went to stay at a neighbor's house.

For the next several days Lucy complained to anyone who would talk with her that Joseph was an impostor who was after her husband's money. At the end of two weeks Martin took her back to Palmyra, where she told people that Joseph was trying to take away everything she owned. She gathered up all of her furniture, bedding, and other belongings and had them all hauled to the homes of her friends.

"I have to protect them from him," she explained.

Martin went back to Harmony, where he stayed from April 12 to June 14, 1828. He worked for Joseph, writing down the translation from the plates. By that time there were some 116 pages of writing. Martin was so impressed that he asked Joseph if he could take the pages to Palmyra with him when he went home to conduct some business.

"I don't think that would be a good idea," Joseph said.

"Ask of the Lord, Joseph," Martin said. "Through the Urim and Thummim."

Joseph felt reluctant to do this. But when Martin continued to coax, he finally did so.

"I'm sorry, Martin," Joseph reported to him later. "The Lord says I must not let these pages go out of my hands."

"But," Martin persisted, "think of what it might mean for your project if I could show the people in Palmyra what you are doing and convince them of its truthfulness. And also," he added, "I would like to show the pages to my wife. Perhaps then she will stop her destructive behavior."

Joseph shook his head.

"Inquire of the Lord again," Martin pleaded. He continued to implore until Joseph agreed to ask once more.

But after he did so, he told Martin, "The answer is still no."

Martin was not content. "Once more," he urged. "Ask once more, please."

Joseph was very hesitant to ask about the pages yet again, but Martin insisted; so Joseph did. This time the answer from the Lord was, "Let him go with them. Only he shall covenant with me that he will show them to but five persons." The five were his wife, her sister, his father, his mother, and his brother.

"Those five only," Joseph told Martin. "You must promise me that."

Martin promised. Packing the 116 pages carefully in his bag, he went on his way.

Back in Palmyra, Lucy Harris was so pleased to be allowed to see the pages that she gave Martin permission to lock them inside her own chest of drawers.

Not long afterwards, while Lucy was away visiting relatives for a few days, Martin decided to show the pages to a good friend despite his promise to Joseph that only five persons were to see them.

When he couldn't find the key to the chest, Martin picked the lock, damaging the drawer. After showing the manuscript to his friend, he put it in his own bureau drawer where he could easily get it the next time he wanted it.

He later showed the manuscript to several other friends, asking each one not to tell the Smith family. He did not want it to get back to Joseph that he had broken his promise.

When Lucy returned and saw the damage to her chest of drawers, she became infuriated. "You'll be sorry that you did this," she stormed. "Put the manuscript back in there, right now."

"No," Martin said.

Lucy stomped away, muttering to herself.

Early one morning Martin received a message from Joseph saying that he had been uneasy about the 116 pages and had come to Palmyra to get them. Joseph asked that Martin bring them immediately to his family's home.

Martin went to his drawer to get the manuscript. But it was not there.

Frantically, Martin searched the house, stirring through every drawer of every chest. "Why are you doing this?" Lucy demanded when she saw him ripping open beds and pillows.

"The 116 pages," Martin cried, tearing a pillow apart and scattering the feathers. "They're missing. I can't find them anywhere." Turning suspiciously to his wife, he said, "Lucy, have you done something with them? Please tell me. I can't face Joseph without them."

"What are you talking about?" Lucy said. "Of course I didn't do anything with them."

Martin continued to search every part of their house. But the pages were not to be found.

His feet felt as heavy as boulders as he started walking to the Smiths' home. When he got to the split-rail fence surrounding their yard, he stopped. Climbing onto the top rail, he settled there, his hat over his face.

How was he ever going to tell Joseph that the 116 pages were lost?

CHAPTER 12

LOST!

Joseph paced anxiously as he waited for Martin Harris to come. The message he'd sent in the early morning said Martin should come as soon as he possibly could. Mother Lucy set a place for him at the breakfast table at 8:00, but he didn't come. "We'll wait to eat until he gets here," Mother Lucy announced.

The rest of the family set about their morning work, but Joseph was so uneasy that he could do nothing but peer out of the windows. He was frantic about the 116 pages and also worried about how things were going back in Harmony.

A few weeks before, on the day after Martin had left to return home, Emma had given birth to a baby boy. The baby died shortly after being born. Joseph had buried him in a small cemetery that he could see from his translation room.

For two weeks Joseph had been afraid for Emma's health. She'd been so ill and depressed that it seemed she might not recover. Joseph had spent all of his time caring for her.

When Emma began to get well, Joseph had thought again about the 116-page manuscript. Why had Martin been gone so long with it without sending back any messages? Had something happened to the manuscript? Emma had been as uneasy as Joseph. She had told him he should go to Palmyra and find out what was happening.

Now, as Joseph stared out of the window of his parents' home near Palmyra, he wished he had never let Martin take the 116 pages.

This time as he looked, Joseph saw Martin perched dejectedly on the fence, his hat down over his face. He carried nothing in his hands.

Something was definitely wrong. But perhaps Martin had left the manuscript at his home in order to keep it safe. Joseph tried to stay calm.

When Martin finally slid down from the fence and slouched on to the house, Mother Lucy greeted him pleasantly. Joseph wanted to demand that Martin tell him about the manuscript, but he held his tongue.

"Come in and sit down, Martin," Mother Lucy said. "We've been waiting until you came to have breakfast."

Not saying a word, Martin took the chair Mother Lucy offered him and sat down at the table. After everyone else was seated, he picked up his knife and fork. Suddenly he dropped them with a clatter.

"Martin," said Mother Lucy, "why do you not eat? Are you sick?"

Martin put his hands to his head, massaging his temples. Suddenly he blurted out, "Oh, I have lost my soul! I have lost my soul!"

Joseph leaped to his feet, knocking his chair backward. "Martin," he cried, "where are the 116 pages? Have you lost the manuscript? Have you broken your oath and brought condemnation upon my head as well as your own?"

Martin hung his head, whispering, "Yes. It is gone, and I know not where."

Joseph groaned and began striding rapidly about the room. "All is lost!" he wailed. "All is lost! What shall I do?"

His mother hurried to his side, but Joseph would not be comforted. "I have sinned," he cried. "It is I who tempted the wrath of God. I should have been satisfied with the first answer I received from the Lord. He told me that it was not safe to let the writing go out of my possession."

In despair, Joseph paced back and forth, back and forth, groaning and berating himself. Finally, he calmed enough to ask Martin to go home and hunt again for the manuscript.

Martin shook his head. "I have ripped everything open in my search. I know it is not there."

"Then must I return to Emma with such a tale as this?" Joseph cried. "I dare not do it." He told the others that the shock might kill her because she was still weak from the birth and loss of their baby.

He went on pacing and mourning until sunset, when his mother talked him into eating some food.

The next morning he said good-bye to his parents and brothers and sisters and set out for Harmony to tell the awful news to Emma. He was only twenty-two years old, but it seemed as if his life was a total disaster.

CHAPTER 13

HEAVENLY VISITORS

Emma was very upset when Joseph got home and told her what had happened. But she told him he must pray for forgiveness. Joseph found a quiet place to kneel and poured out his heart to God, asking to be forgiven of everything he had done wrong.

Soon an angel stood before him and told him he had wearied the Lord with his pleas to let Martin take the manuscript. As a result, Joseph became responsible for what Martin did with it. Since the manuscript was lost, the angel said, Joseph would have to suffer the consequences. The angel took away the golden plates and the Urim and Thummim.

Joseph felt horrible but was willing to do whatever the Lord asked in order to be forgiven. As the days went by, he continued to pray and did all that he could to repent.

He was so repentant that the angel appeared again and let him use the Urim and Thummim briefly to receive a revelation. In it, the Lord reminded Joseph that the works and purposes of God cannot be stopped or brought to nothing. After scolding Joseph severely, the Lord declared, "But remember, God is merciful; therefore, repent of that which thou hast done which is contrary to the commandment which I gave you, and thou art still chosen, and art again called to the work."

Soon after this revelation, the golden plates and the Urim and Thummim were given back to Joseph. The angel told Joseph that the Lord loved him for his faithfulness and humility.

Joseph was so relieved and excited to be given a second chance that he planned to spend day and night on the translation. But through the Urim and Thummim he received another revelation telling him not to run faster or labor more than he had strength.

The Lord also warned Joseph that those who now had possession of the stolen manuscript pages would be prompted by Satan to change the words. Joseph was told not to retranslate the pages because the evil men would show their changed version and scoff at Joseph because the words were different.

After receiving this revelation, Joseph did not do any translating for a while. Instead, he dedicated his time to providing for his family by working on the farm he planned to buy from Emma's parents.

When he did begin translating again, Emma served as his scribe. But she was too busy with household duties to work full time with him. The Lord told Joseph that He would send him a scribe, and Joseph waited patiently for the promise to be fulfilled.

In February 1829 his parents came from Palmyra to visit. They were happy to find Joseph feeling much more cheerful than the last time they'd seen him. Joseph told them everything was going well except that he really needed a scribe. He told them about the Lord's promise to send him one.

Soon after his parents returned home, a young man named Oliver Cowdery came to teach school in Palmyra. He boarded at the Smith home, and when he heard about Joseph's work, he was impressed. He felt strongly that he should go to visit Joseph. "If there is a work for me to do in this thing," he said, "I am determined to attend to it."

After the school term ended, Oliver set out for Pennsylvania with Joseph's

brother Samuel. The weather had been very wet and cold so that the roads were deep with mud. It was almost impossible to travel. But this did not stop Oliver.

Because Joseph had prayed for a scribe, he was not even surprised when Oliver arrived, offering to help. The two men sat down and talked until late in the night. Both marveled at the ways of the Lord and how He had brought them together.

On April 7, 1829, Joseph started translating with Oliver Cowdery serving as his scribe. The two of them worked very well as a team.

Joseph worried a lot about taking care of his family since the translating took up almost all of his time. But Emma did not complain, even though supplies were getting low.

The scripture Joseph translated was divided into books, like the Bible. It told the story of people who left Jerusalem to go to a new land across the sea and what happened to them there. It described two great tribes of people, the Nephites and the Lamanites. As the work went on, Joseph and Oliver learned that the Savior himself had visited these people in the new land, after His crucifixion. The Savior taught them the principles of His gospel and established His church among them.

Joseph and Oliver were especially interested in what He had said about baptism. "I give unto you power that ye shall baptize this people," the Savior had said, "when I am again ascended into heaven."

Clearly, this meant that baptism must be performed by someone who had the authority to do so. Joseph and Oliver talked about it and decided that no one in their day held this authority. Only God could restore it to earth.

The two men prayed to know how they could bring about the restoration of the priesthood authority. It wasn't long before they found out.

One morning as they sat down to work, a commandment came through the Urim and Thummim. It told Joseph and Oliver to be baptized.

They still weren't sure exactly what to do. So on May 15, 1829, they went into the woods to pray for further knowledge. As they prayed, a messenger from heaven came down in a shaft of light. The angel identified himself as John, who had been called John the Baptist in the New Testament. It had been he who baptized Jesus in the River Jordan.

The angel laid his hands upon their heads, saying, "Upon you my fellow servants, in the name of Messiah, I confer the Priesthood of Aaron, which holds the keys of the ministering of angels, and of the gospel of repentance, and of baptism by immersion for the remission of sins; and this shall never be taken again from the earth, until the sons of Levi do offer again an offering unto the Lord in righteousness."

John said he acted under the direction of Peter, James, and John, who held the keys of the Priesthood of Melchizedek, which Joseph and Oliver would later receive. He told them they should now go into the water and be baptized. Joseph was to baptize Oliver, then Oliver was to baptize Joseph, under the authority of the new priesthood they had received.

They hurried to the nearby Susquehanna River, where they waded into the water and baptized each other, as they'd been told to do. Then, as instructed by the angel, Joseph laid his hands on Oliver's head and ordained him to the Aaronic Priesthood. Oliver did the same for Joseph.

After this spiritual experience, Joseph and Oliver found that their understanding of their work greatly increased. The meanings of scripture passages were made much clearer to them. They were so excited that they wanted to shout it out to all the world.

However, they could tell only a few close and trusted friends. There was a spirit of persecution building up around them. There were threats of mobs coming to destroy what they were doing. They had to be very careful.

In the meantime, Joseph's brother Samuel expressed curiosity about their work. Joseph and Oliver showed him some of the translation. They tried to convince him that the gospel of Jesus Christ was about to be revealed in its fulness.

Samuel didn't believe what they said. "This can't be true," he said. "It's too preposterous."

"If we can't convince you," Joseph told him, "then God will. Ask Him if what we say is true."

Samuel agreed to do this. Going alone into the woods, he prayed fervently to know the truth. When he returned to Joseph's house, he said he wanted to be baptized.

Not long afterward, Joseph's older brother Hyrum came to visit. He, too, believed and would soon be baptized.

By now supplies at the Smith home were very low, and it looked as if Joseph and Oliver would have to stop translating in order to earn some money. Then one day Joseph Knight, an old friend of the Smith family, arrived with a wagon full of food and also some writing paper. "I don't want you to interrupt your work," he told Joseph. "It is too important."

Though he lived nearly thirty miles away and had to travel by horse and wagon, Mr. Knight came several times to bring bushels of grain and potatoes and a barrel of salted mackerel so that Joseph could continue his work.

Joseph was anxious to finish the translation as soon as possible. Rumors spoke of mobs being formed to stop the work. Some people threatened to do him harm. Mother Lucy later wrote that "evil-designing people were seeking to take away his life, in order to prevent the work of God from going forth to the world."

Joseph knew that other things must happen too. When John the Baptist had bestowed the Aaronic Priesthood upon him and Oliver, he had spoken of a greater priesthood after the order of Melchizedek that would soon be given to them. This priesthood would give them the necessary keys and authority to organize the true church at a time that would soon be revealed.

One day, probably in May 1829, just as John had promised, Peter, James, and John did indeed appear to Joseph and Oliver between Harmony and Colesville where Joseph Knight lived. The exact date of this restoration is not known, nor is the exact place where it occurred.

The important thing is that it happened. Peter, James, and John, ancient apostles of Jesus Christ, laid their hands on the heads of the two men and bestowed the Melchizedek Priesthood, restoring to the earth authority that would be needed to reorganize and operate Christ's church.

This restoration placed a heavy responsibility on Joseph and Oliver, but they accepted it with joy and returned to their work of translation with renewed determination and urgency.

CHAPTER 14

A Surprising Message

Day after day Joseph went on with the work of translating the golden plates. Using the Urim and Thummim, he was able to translate the meaning of the engravings. Oliver wrote down everything Joseph said.

Their friend Joseph Knight continued to bring supplies for them and Emma. Joseph's younger brother Samuel, who had brought Oliver to Harmony, helped by doing much of the work on the farm. Before long, however, he returned to Palmyra.

Life became difficult for Joseph. He needed to work on the translation, but he had to support Emma and now Oliver too. The supplies he received were generous but not enough to allow them to work without worrying. Also, there were still people lurking about, looking for ways to prevent Joseph from going on with the translation.

One day Joseph received inspiration through the Urim and Thummim that he should send a letter to a man by the name of David Whitmer in Fayette, near Palmyra. He was to ask Mr. Whitmer to come to Harmony immediately with a team of horses and a wagon to carry Joseph and Oliver to the Whitmer home, where they would finish the translation. Otherwise, evil men might take

Joseph's life to keep him from completing his work. Oliver wrote the letter, as they had been instructed, and sent it off.

When David Whitmer received the letter asking him to come to Pennsylvania, he showed it to his family. "What do you think I should do about it?" he asked.

"Why, David, you're right in the midst of a big job," his father said. "You know you have sowed as much wheat as you can harrow in tomorrow and the next day, and then you have a quantity of plaster of paris to spread that is much needed on your land."

Oliver wrote down everything Joseph said.

David's father, being a very religious man, also said that David could not do what Joseph asked unless God gave him evidence that he should.

This suggestion made good sense to David. He prayed, asking the Lord for a testimony about what was asked of him. He was told by the voice of the Spirit to harrow in his wheat, then go immediately to Pennsylvania.

The next morning David gazed out over the field and estimated that it would take at least two days of heavy work to finish what needed to be done. He told himself that if he was able to do this work faster than it had ever been done before, that would be a sure sign it was the Lord's will that he help Joseph Smith.

Hitching his horses to the harrow, he began working. At noon, when he stopped for dinner, he discovered to his surprise that half the field was done. After dinner he went on as before, and by evening he had completed what should have taken two days to accomplish.

When his father saw that the work was finished, he exclaimed, "There must be an overruling hand in this. I think you had better go down to Pennsylvania as soon as the plaster of paris is spread."

The next morning when David went out to spread the plaster, he discovered it was gone. Two days before, he had left two large heaps of it near his sister's house. But now there was nothing but bare ground.

He ran inside the house to find his sister. "What happened to the piles of plaster of paris that I left here?" he asked. "Did someone take it?"

Her eyebrows went up. "Why do you ask me?" she said. "Wasn't it all spread yesterday?"

"Not to my knowledge," David said.

His sister went to the window and looked out where the piles had been. "I am astonished at that," his sister said. "The children came in yesterday morning and begged me to go out and see the men in the field. They said they had never seen anyone spread plaster so fast in all their lives."

Bewildered, David asked if she had gone out to look.

She nodded. "I saw three men at work, just as the children said. I supposed that you had hired someone to help since I knew you were in a hurry to get it done. So I thought no more about it."

"I hired no one," David said. "Perhaps some of the neighbors did it for me."

But when he went around the neighborhood to thank whoever had done it, he found that no one knew a thing about it.

David marveled at the miraculous way his work had been done. It convinced both him and his father even more that he should do what Joseph had asked.

David started out immediately. His horses were sturdy and energetic, and he was able to travel more than forty miles the first day. He also made good time on the second day of travel. On the third day, to his surprise, he met Joseph and Oliver on the road.

"We have come to greet you," they told him.

As the three of them headed on to Joseph's house, Oliver took David aside when they stopped to rest the horses. "Joseph told me the exact time you left your house," he said. "He also told me where you stopped to water your horses and where you ate lunch."

David was puzzled. "How did Joseph know these things?"

Oliver replied, "I do not know, but I kept a record of what he said." He showed the record to David. Everything was accurate. This miracle increased David's faith that Joseph Smith was indeed a prophet. He was happy to have Joseph and Oliver come to his father's house to live while they worked on the translation.

Joseph was pleased to be able to go there and said he and Oliver would pack up immediately. As he prepared to go, he asked the Lord what he should do with the golden plates. He received the answer that he should give them to an angel, who would return them to him at the Whitmer farm. The angel came, and Joseph delivered the plates to him.

After saying good-bye to Emma, who would follow them soon, David, Joseph, and Oliver started on their journey to New York. On the way they saw an aged man walking along the road. The man raised his hat and rubbed his brow as if he were too warm. "Good morning," he said to them.

"Good morning," they replied.

They noticed that he carried a knapsack on his back, and from the way he walked, it seemed very heavy.

"Ask him to ride," Joseph told David.

David politely asked the man if he would like to come and ride in the wagon.

"No," he said. "I am just going over to Cumorah."

Puzzled, David turned to Joseph and said, "Cumorah? I know all the country around here, but I've never heard of Cumorah. What's he talking about?"

When he turned back, the man was gone. "What does this mean?" he demanded.

Joseph looked a little pale. "The man was a Nephite. The bundle he carried contained the golden plates." It was the angel who had taken the plates from Joseph for safekeeping.

David Whitmer marveled that he should be part of this miraculous work.

When they reached the Whitmer farm, the angel returned the plates as promised. The very next day, Joseph and Oliver continued the translation. Oliver served as scribe most of the time, although other people helped.

It was a great relief to work among friendly people. Joseph and Oliver hoped they could stay there with the Whitmers until the translation was complete.

CHAPTER 15

WITNESSES OF THE GOLDEN PLATES

Joseph and Oliver were warmly welcomed at the Whitmer home, but it was hard for Mrs. Whitmer to have them there. She had a large family of sons with just one daughter living at home to help with all the housework. The two of them had to prepare all the meals, plant and tend the garden, bake the bread, churn the butter, make and mend the clothing, and do much of the other work on the farm. Mrs. Whitmer did not complain, but she wasn't sure she could take care of two more people.

One day she felt very discouraged as she went out to milk the cows. Before long she came back to the house filled with joy. When asked why she looked so happy, she replied, "I have seen the messenger." She went on to say that she had come upon an elderly man out near the barn. Her description of him showed he was the same man with the knapsack that Joseph, Oliver, and David had seen on their journey from Pennsylvania.

Mrs. Whitmer said the man told her that she would be blessed for providing a safe place for Joseph and Oliver to work. Then he took out the golden plates and showed them to her. "They were fastened together with rings on the right side," she told her family, "so that the pages would turn over from left to right." The man turned several of the plates, leaf by leaf.

She, Mary Musselman Whitmer, was the first person besides Joseph to actually see the golden plates. Seeing them was her own personal reward for taking care of Joseph and Oliver. But soon other people would see them for a different purpose, to be witnesses to the world.

As soon as he could, Joseph went on with the translation. One day he came upon this passage: "And behold, ye may be privileged that ye may show the plates unto those who shall assist to bring forth this work; And unto three shall they be shown by the power of God."

Joseph was excited by these words, written centuries earlier as a message to the translator of the plates, who was himself. Three special witnesses would be provided by the Lord. They were to bear witness to the world that they had seen the golden plates and that the Book of Mormon had been translated from the writings they contained.

Oliver, who was serving as scribe at the time the words were written, was also inspired by the Lord's promise. Martin Harris had come by the Whitmer home to see how the translation was progressing, and soon Martin and Oliver, together with David Whitmer, asked Joseph if they could be the three special witnesses.

Joseph asked the Lord through the Urim and Thummim and received an answer. The Lord promised Oliver, David, and Martin that if they relied on Him "with full purpose of heart," they would see the plates and other sacred objects. After Joseph received this revelation, Oliver, David, and Martin knew they had to prepare themselves for this blessing and wait for the proper time.

As soon as Joseph completed the translation, the angel came and took the plates again. Not many days after receiving the revelation about the three witnesses, Joseph sent a letter to his parents, asking them to come to Fayette. They came, bringing Martin Harris with them. They were all amazed and impressed at what Joseph had accomplished.

The next day, after breakfast, the Whitmer family and the visitors held morning services, reading, singing, and praying. When they rose from their knees, Joseph put his hand on Martin's shoulder. "Martin Harris," he said, "you have to humble yourself before your God this day and obtain a forgiveness for your sins. If you will do this, it is God's will that you and Oliver Cowdery and David Whitmer should look upon the plates."

The three men were delighted. The time had come for them to receive the promised blessing. Soon afterward, they went with Joseph to the woods, where they knelt and began to pray fervently. Joseph prayed first, with the others following in turn.

Nothing happened.

They tried again, each one taking his turn being the voice for the prayers.

Still nothing happened.

Martin Harris rose from his knees. "I think I should take myself away," he said. "Perhaps my presence is the cause of our not obtaining what we wish for."

Before the others could object, he walked off into the trees.

Joseph, Oliver, and David began praying again. In a short time they saw a very bright light, and an angel stood before them. In his hands he held the plates.

Slowly, as they watched, the angel turned the pages, one by one, so they could see the engravings on them. A voice came out of the light, saying, "These plates have been revealed by the power of God, and they have been translated by the power of God. The translation of them which you have seen is correct, and I command you to bear record of what you now see and hear."

When the light faded, Oliver and David felt so weak that they needed to rest. But Joseph rose and went in search of Martin Harris. He found him a considerable distance away, still engaged in fervent prayer.

"I haven't yet been privileged to see anything," he told Joseph. "Perhaps it would help for you to pray with me."

Joseph agreed, and the two of them beseeched the Lord to allow Martin to see the plates.

Time passed. Then suddenly the light came, and Martin saw the same vision that the others had seen. He was overcome with joy. "It is enough," he rejoiced. "Mine eyes have beheld!"

The four men, Joseph, Oliver, Martin, and David, now returned to the house, where Joseph sought out his parents. "Father, Mother," he said, "you do not know how happy I am. The Lord has now caused the plates to be shown to three more besides myself."

His parents rose up to embrace him and share his joy.

"The three men were told," Joseph continued, "that they will bear witness to the truth of what I have said, for now they know for themselves that I do not go about to deceive people. I feel as if I was relieved of a burden which was almost too heavy for me to bear."

The following day Joseph's parents and Martin returned home to Palmyra. In a few days Joseph, Oliver, and the Whitmers joined them there. They came to discuss arrangements to get the Book of Mormon printed.

Soon after they arrived, Joseph took eight of the men with him to a special place nearby where members of the Smith family often went to pray. Joseph had been told that an angel would carry the golden plates there. When they reached the spot, Joseph allowed the eight witnesses to see and touch the plates. The eight witnesses were David Whitmer's brothers Christian, Jacob, Peter Junior, and John, David's brother-in-law Hiram Page, and two of Joseph's brothers, Hyrum and Samuel, as well as their father, Joseph Senior.

That evening the whole group held a meeting in the Smith's log home at which all of the witnesses—the three and the eight—bore testimony of what they had seen. They all testified that the latter-day dispensation of the gospel had been ushered in.

Later the two sets of witnesses would write testimonies of what they had seen. These testimonies appear in every Book of Mormon ever printed by the Church.

CHAPTER 16

PUBLISHING THE BOOK OF MORMON

After the translation work was finished, Joseph faced other problems. How was he going to get the Book of Mormon published? Printing it would cost a lot of money. He had no money. And what printer would agree to do it? Many people did not want what they called "Joe Smith's gold bible" to be published. It was possible that they would try to destroy the manuscript and even harm Joseph.

The first printer Joseph approached in Palmyra was Egbert Bratt Grandin, publisher of a local newspaper. "I can't even consider printing the book," Mr. Grandin said. "If I did, people would say I believe it is true. I don't want them to think that."

Eventually Joseph found a publisher in Rochester who agreed to do the printing for the money his friend Martin Harris promised to provide.

Now Joseph went back to Mr. Grandin. "I have found a printer who is willing to do what I want," he told him. "You are losing a good business opportunity if you don't do it because we will sell a lot of copies of the Book of Mormon here in Palmyra."

The first printer Joseph approached in Palmyra was Egbert Bratt Grandin.

Mr. Grandin thought about it. He talked with some of his neighbors. They said it was all right with them if he published the book just for the money.

"I will do the printing," Mr. Grandin told Joseph.

By August 25, 1829, Martin Harris arranged for a mortgage on his farm to get the money. He signed papers promising to pay Mr. Grandin the sum of $3,000 for the printing of 5,000 copies of the Book of Mormon.

On the morning Joseph planned to sign the contract with Mr. Grandin, Dr. McIntyre, who had always been friendly to the Smiths, came hurrying to their home. "You must not leave the house today, Joseph," he said breathlessly. "There is a mob of about forty men waiting to pounce on you. They plan to beat you up and stop you from going on with the publication of your book."

Mother Lucy put a hand to her mouth. "Oh no," she gasped.

Joseph strode to a window and looked out. "Are you sure of this? How did you find out?"

"They came to me," Dr. McIntyre told him. "They asked me to take command of the group. I refused to do it, and Mr. Huzzy said he would take charge. They are gathered in the woods now, a short distance down the road."

"Joseph," Mother Lucy said, "you must not go now. Wait until your father and brothers come in from the fields to protect you."

Joseph looked out of the window again. "Never mind, Mother," he said. "Just put your trust in God. Nothing will hurt me today." He prepared to leave.

"I'll accompany you," Dr. McIntyre said. "You must not go alone."

Joseph shook his head. "I don't want you to get involved in this, my friend. You have helped enough already. You wait here with Mother so she will feel safe."

Without listening to further objections, Joseph left the house, keeping an eye out for the mob. He walked some distance before he saw them roosting like a row of crows on a fence surrounding a neighbor's field. They watched as he approached.

Politely removing his hat, Joseph greeted Mr. Huzzy, who sat at the head of the line. "Good morning," he said. "Fine day, isn't it?" He went on down the line, calling each man by name and saying a few pleasant words to each one. Then, leaving the confused and amazed men staring after him, he continued on to Palmyra, where he signed all the necessary papers to start the printing of the Book of Mormon.

When he returned home, he said, "Well, Mother, did I not tell you that I should be delivered from the hands of all my enemies? They were there, all right, all mustered together and perched on the fence. But they went home, and I'll warrant you they wish they had stayed there in the first place!"

Weeks before, Joseph had registered the copyright of the Book of Mormon, which meant the book was legally his and that other people couldn't copy large parts of it without his permission. With that done and the printing contract arranged, Joseph could finally go home to the little house near Emma's parents.

"I am going back to Pennsylvania," he told Oliver. "I want you to stay here in Palmyra to watch over the printing of the book."

Before he left, Joseph received a revelation that contained these instructions from the Lord: First, Oliver Cowdery should make a copy of the entire manuscript. Second, he should take only one copy at a time to the printing office, so that if one copy was destroyed, there would still be another. Third, whenever Oliver went to and from the printing office, he should have a guard with him to protect the manuscript. Fourth, a guard should stand watch at the Smith home both night and day in case someone came to destroy the manuscript.

After making sure that Oliver knew what he was supposed to do, Joseph set out on the long journey to Harmony, Pennsylvania.

For a while things went well in Palmyra. Oliver took about a dozen pages of the copied manuscript to the printing office each day. He stayed there to proofread each finished page.

But as the pages of the book came off the printing press, men from various religions in the town began to drop by the printing office. One day they met together in a room next to the one in which Oliver and a young man named Robinson were working. Mr. Robinson, curious about what they were saying, put his ear to the wall between the rooms.

"They're worried about how the Book of Mormon will affect other churches here in Palmyra," he reported to Oliver. "They're afraid it might take people away from them. They've all agreed they can't let that happen."

He listened some more, then told Oliver that they were making plans to prevent the printing of the book. "Some of them are going to stop by the Smith home," Mr. Robinson said. "They plan to ask Mrs. Smith to read to them from the manuscript. They'll divert her attention in some way, then grab the manuscript and throw it into the fire."

When Oliver went to the Smith home that evening, he told Mother Lucy all he had learned.

"I'm glad for the warning," Mother Lucy said.

She then placed the manuscript in a large chest. "Oliver," she said, "please lift up the head of my bed."

When he did, she shoved the chest underneath. When the bed was let down, it rested firmly on the lid of the chest.

"There's no way they can take the manuscript from me," Mother Lucy stated.

Four days later, three men came to visit Mother Lucy soon after her husband had left the house. She invited them to come in and sit down. The men were an official committee sent by the church she had once joined. She didn't know if they were the men planning to burn the manuscript, but she didn't take any chances.

After they were seated, one of the men said, "Mrs. Smith, we hear that you have a gold bible. We have come to see if you will be so kind as to show it to us."

"Why, no, gentlemen," she said. "We have no gold bible. But we do have a translation of some gold plates."

She told them what was contained in the manuscript. She compared the religious teachings in it to what was taught in the New Testament. "Why should anyone be alarmed by this?" she asked. "Is it merely because they fear their religions will suffer a loss of members? Do the ministers tremble for their salaries? Do they rage because the book clarifies some principles beyond the knowledge they have?"

The men were silent for a time. Then one of them asked, "Well, may we just see the manuscript?"

"No, sir," she replied. "You may not see it. I have told you what it contains. That must be enough."

The three men looked at one another. One named Mr. Beckwith said, "Mrs. Smith, you and most of your children have belonged to our church for some time. We respect you very highly and cannot bear the thoughts of losing you."

The other men nodded, and Mr. Beckwith went on. "We can see that you believe much of what your son has told you. If you do believe those things, we wish that you would not say anything that might influence others to read the book."

"Deacon Beckwith," Mother Lucy said. "If you should stick my flesh full of fiery sticks and even burn me at the stake, I would still declare that Joseph has got that record and that I know it to be true."

Mr. Beckwith turned to his companions. "You see it is of no use to say anything more to her."

The three men said polite farewells and went outside. There they found Hyrum chopping wood. "Mr. Smith," Mr. Beckwith said, "do you not think that you may be deceived about that record which your brother pretends to have found?"

Hyrum stopped his work. "No sir," he said. "I do not."

"Well now," Mr. Beckwith persisted, "if you did find that you are deceived and that he found no such record, will you confess the fact to me?"

Hyrum smiled. "Mr. Beckwith, when the book is printed, will you take one and read it, asking God to give you an evidence that you may know whether it is true?"

Mr. Beckwith looked startled. "I think it beneath me to take so much trouble." He hesitated, then said, "But yes, if you will promise what I asked, I will pray for a witness whether or not the book is true."

Then, still smiling pleasantly, Hyrum said, "This is what I'll do, Mr. Beckwith. If you do get a testimony from God that the book is not true, then I will confess to you that it is not true."

They shook hands to seal this agreement, and the men left peaceably. They didn't bother the Smiths again.

Hyrum and Oliver soon discovered that a man named Abner Cole was going to the print shop on Sundays to put out his own newspaper, called *The Reflector.* While there, he was copying parts of the Book of Mormon and including them in his paper, giving them to people so they could read the book without paying for it.

This worried Joseph's friends for two reasons. First, it was illegal. Second, Martin Harris had put up money to pay for the printing. They needed to sell the book so Martin could get his money back.

In addition to parts of the Book of Mormon, *The Reflector* also contained crude, disgusting articles that Mr. Cole wrote himself under the made-up name Obediah Dogberry. When Hyrum and Oliver tried to stop him from printing parts of the Book of Mormon in his disgraceful paper, Mr. Cole said, "It is none of your business. I have hired the press on Sundays, and I will print what I please."

Father Joseph went to bring Joseph back from Harmony to take care of the problem. When Joseph came, he confronted Mr. Cole. "I have a copyright on the Book of Mormon and you cannot legally use any parts of it," he said.

Angrily, Mr. Cole removed his coat. Rolling up the sleeves of his shirt, he doubled up his fists. "Do you want to fight, sir?" he roared at Joseph. "I will publish what I please. If you want to fight, just come on."

Mr. Cole looked so silly that Joseph smiled. "Mr. Cole," he said, "keep your coat on. It is cold, and I am not going to fight you. Nevertheless, you have got to stop printing my book, for I know my rights."

Mr. Cole continued to dance around with his fists raised. "If you think you are the best man," he bawled, "show it."

Joseph shook his head. "Mr. Cole," he said in a soft voice, "there is law, and you will find that out, if you do not understand it. But I shall not fight you, sir."

Mr. Cole began to cool off now. He knew that Joseph had properly filed for a copyright. Grumbling, he put his coat back on.

But there was still more trouble. Some of the people in the area got together and vowed that none of them or their families would buy copies of the Book of Mormon. This frightened the printer, Mr. Grandin, because he thought he might not get paid for his work.

When Joseph asked of the Lord what should be done, he received a revelation that Martin Harris should pay Mr. Grandin the money they owed. Although Martin was worried that he might never get his money back if the book did not sell, he went to Mr. Grandin and assured him that the bill would be paid. This satisfied Mr. Grandin, and the printing of the Book of Mormon went on.

CHAPTER 17

THE CHURCH IS ORGANIZED

After Joseph and Oliver received the Aaronic Priesthood on May 15, 1829, they began preaching the gospel to a few friends and family members who would listen. Their neighbors in Pennsylvania were not friendly, but when they moved to the Whitmer home in New York, they found many opportunities to teach interested people.

Over time, many people believed their words, and some were baptized.

Joseph and Oliver traveled around as much as they could, spreading encouragement and telling the believers what was happening.

One day in June 1829, they were praying together in a room at the Whitmer home. Suddenly they heard a voice commanding Joseph to ordain Oliver to be an elder in the Church of Jesus Christ. The voice said Oliver should then ordain Joseph to the same office, and they should go on to ordain others. They also received other instructions on organizing the Church.

A long time passed before they could obey the instructions in the revelation.

During this time, the Book of Mormon was being printed. While he waited for it, Joseph received many other revelations. One of these pointed out that

April 6, 1830, was the day when the Church of Jesus Christ should again be organized on the earth.

When April 6 came, many of Joseph's friends and neighbors, including several who had already been baptized, gathered at the Whitmers' house. Joseph was excited that day and enthusiastically welcomed everyone who came.

After a prayer, he asked the assembled brethren to vote whether they would accept those who would be ordained as their teachers in the things of the Kingdom of God. If so, he told them, they would go ahead and organize the Church according to the commandment he had received.

Everybody voted yes.

The law said that there must be not fewer than three and not more than nine official organizers. Six of the men present, including Joseph, Hyrum, and Oliver, were chosen to be the Church's first official members.

As he had been instructed to do, Joseph laid his hands on Oliver's head and ordained him an elder. Oliver, in turn, laid his hands on Joseph and ordained him.

After this was done, the two of them took bread, blessed and broke it, and passed it around for all present to eat. Then they blessed and passed around wine so all could drink in memory of Jesus, as had been done in Bible times. Later, the Lord gave a revelation that allowed the use of water instead of wine.

The next thing to do was to lay their hands on all those present who had been baptized to confirm them members of the Church and give them the gift of the Holy Ghost.

There was such an outpouring of the Spirit that a number of people present, including Joseph's own parents and Martin Harris, soon came forward to ask for baptism. Joseph's father and Martin Harris were baptized that very evening, and Joseph's mother two or three days later.

Joseph stood on the shore to watch his father be baptized. When his father came out of the water, Joseph cried with joy. "Oh, my God," he said, addressing Heavenly Father, "have I lived to see my own father baptized into the true church of Jesus Christ?"

The great work of the Church had now begun.

Right away there were problems to solve. Many people questioned whether they needed to go through a second baptism if they had already been baptized in another church. This question was answered by a revelation in which the Lord declared that all old covenants had been done away. People did indeed need to be baptized again as members of the restored Church of Jesus Christ.

Another problem brought about the first miracle through the use of the powers of the restored priesthood. At the early meetings of the Church, the group prayed aloud a lot. Newel Knight, son of the Smith family's long-time friend Joseph Knight, had trouble with this. When Joseph asked him to pray aloud, he would excuse himself, saying he couldn't do it. Joseph offered to help him, but Newel refused.

One day Joseph had a talk with Newel. "Brother Newel," he said, "if you were to get into a mud-hole, would you not try to get yourself out?"

Puzzled as to what Joseph was getting at, Newel answered, "Yes, of course."

"Well," Joseph said, "if I and some of the other brethren came along and were willing to help you out of the mud-hole, would you not let us assist you?"

Now Newel understood what Joseph meant. "Joseph," he said, "if I had got into the mud-hole though carelessness, I would rather wait and get out myself than to have others help me." He told Joseph that he would practice praying so that he could get used to it.

The next day he went into the woods, where he made several attempts to pray aloud but found he couldn't do it. He thought about the many times he had refused to pray in the presence of the other members. The more he thought about it, the worse he felt, in both mind and body. He decided to go home, but by the time he got there he looked so terrible that his wife was alarmed. "Why, what is the matter?" she asked.

Newel's face and body were beginning to twist and twitch. "Go get Joseph Smith," he managed to say.

When Joseph came, he, too, was alarmed. Newel's face and limbs were contorted now, and it was as if something lifted him up and tossed him across the room.

His wife had told other friends and relatives when she was out, and soon several were gathered to see what could be done.

Joseph, trying to calm him, grasped him firmly by the hand. "Tell me what is happening," he urged.

Newel's mouth was so twisted he could hardly speak, but he managed to say that the devil was in him. "Please cast him out," he pleaded. "I know that you can do it."

"If you know that I can," Joseph said, "it shall be done." With his new priesthood authority, he rebuked the devil and commanded him in the name of Jesus Christ to depart from Newel's body.

Almost immediately, Newel's agitation ceased. "I saw him leave and vanish from my sight," he said feebly. His face became natural again and his body stopped twitching. But he was so weak that he had to be helped to his bed, where he lay for some time.

When he was able to sit up and speak, he told those present that the Spirit of the Lord had descended upon him after Joseph had commanded the devil to depart. He said visions of eternity had been opened to his view.

This was so impressive to those who had witnessed it that most of them became members of the Church.

CHAPTER 18

THE CHURCH GROWS AMIDST PERSECUTION

Soon after the Church was organized, all of Joseph's brothers were ordained to the priesthood. Before returning to the home and farm he was buying from Emma's parents in Harmony, Pennsylvania, Joseph called his brother Samuel to be a missionary. In the middle of April 1830, Samuel started through the neighboring towns, beginning a mission to tell people about the newly organized Church and the recently published Book of Mormon.

Months later, after Joseph and Emma had moved to Fayette, they joined Joseph's parents and their family one evening to hear Samuel report on his missionary work.

"How did it go, Samuel?" Joseph asked.

Samuel grinned. "I'll let you decide about that. When I first started out, people rejected what I had to say. But I kept going. After a while, I found a man who bought a copy of the Book of Mormon from me."

"Wonderful!" Joseph exclaimed. "Tell us about him."

Samuel leaned forward in his chair, holding a copy of the book in his hands. "His name is Phineas Young. I met him at an inn when I stopped to have a meal. Since he was very friendly, I showed him the book and said, 'This is something I wish you to read, sir.'"

Emma, who was knitting as she listened, broke in. "Did he take to it right off?"

"No," Samuel said, "he wanted to know what book it was. I told him, 'It's the Book of Mormon, or as some call it, the Golden Bible.' 'Hmm,' he said, 'I've heard tell of it. Purports to be a revelation, doesn't it?' 'Yes,' says I. 'A revelation from God to a man named Joseph Smith, Junior.' Mr. Young took the book and flipped through it. 'And what is your name, young man?' he said. 'Samuel Smith, sir,' I confessed."

Joseph was enjoying Samuel's story. "So what did he say then, Sam?"

"Well," Samuel said, "he rubbed his chin and said, 'Smith, eh? Related to Joseph?' And I said, 'A brother, sir.'" Samuel hefted a copy of the Book of Mormon as he went on with the story. "He seemed to think about that for a while. Then he saw my name, Samuel H. Smith, there in the book and he said, 'Ah, you are one of the witnesses. You say you saw the golden plates?' And I said, 'Yes sir, I did, and I know the book to be a revelation from God and my brother Joseph to be a prophet. If you will read this book with a prayerful heart, you will know the truth of it.' I thought for sure he would hand the book right back to me. But he just smiled a little and said, 'All right, Samuel Smith, I'll buy this book.' And he did."

Emma paused in her knitting, and Joseph clapped his hands together. "Wonderful, Sam," he said. "You're a fine missionary. Who else bought a book?"

Samuel looked a bit sheepish. "Nobody," he said. "That's the only book I sold. Nobody else was interested; so I came home to help with the farm work for a while."

"Well, it's a good start," declared Joseph. "Did you go out again?"

Samuel nodded. "Yes, at the end of June, I headed out again. But I was even less successful than on my first trip."

"What do you mean?" Joseph asked.

"I was driven away from many houses," he replied. "I was spat upon and cursed. Hardly anyone wanted to listen."

Joseph put an arm about Samuel's shoulders. "I'm sorry, Sam," he said. "But you did your best."

Samuel slumped, then raised his head. "I did leave one book with a man named Mr. Greene who was setting out on a preaching circuit. He agreed to show it to the people he met. When I went back to see him, he wasn't home, but his wife, Rhoda, handed me the book. She said her husband didn't find anyone who was interested. But she said she had read it and felt very good about it."

"So you did sell another copy!" Joseph said.

Samuel shook his head. "She didn't have any money, so I gave the book to her. I'm sorry, Joseph. But I just felt that I should."

Joseph clapped him on the shoulder. "You did right, Sam. You never know where that book will get to."

Samuel's downcast face brightened. "As a matter of fact, Mrs. Greene said she wanted to pass it along to some of her family. When we got to talking about that, I found that she's a sister to Phineas Young, the man I sold a book to on my last trip. She said she wants to talk to him about it, and see that her sister Fanny gets to read it. And there's another brother she thinks would be interested. His name is Brigham. Brigham Young."

Joseph was pleased with Samuel's efforts and with the progress the Church was making. More missionaries were called to spread the word. New members told their friends, some of whom were baptized, and they in turn told their friends about the Church.

But as the membership grew, so did the persecution. In June 1830, Joseph, Emma, and some other Church members traveled to the home of their old friend Joseph Knight in Colesville, New York. Joseph had learned that a number of people there wished to be baptized.

After Joseph arrived, he set up a meeting for Sunday. On Saturday, to prepare for the baptisms, he and others built a dam across a creek to create a pond. But during the night, someone came and destroyed the dam.

"We will go ahead with the meeting anyway," Joseph said.

On Monday he and his friends repaired the dam and baptized thirteen people. These included Emma, who had not been baptized previously. While the baptizing was still going on, a mob began to gather. About fifty men watched the proceedings, threatening violence and shouting questions. Joseph answered politely. Eventually the mob left.

That evening Joseph planned a meeting to confirm those who had been baptized earlier in the day. They had just started the meeting when a constable appeared at the door. "I have a warrant for your arrest," he said, holding up a folded paper.

"On what charge?" Joseph asked.

The constable consulted the paper. "On the charge of being a disorderly person," he read, "and of setting the country in an uproar by preaching about the Book of Mormon." He raised his eyes to Joseph, who stood there calm and unresisting. "I have to arrest you," he said, almost apologetically.

"Take me where you must," Joseph said.

Remarking that Joseph was a different kind of person than he'd expected, the constable said, "I want to warn you, Mr. Smith, that a mob is lying in ambush down the road. But I will do my best to protect you."

He asked Joseph to get into his wagon, and they started off. They hadn't gone very far when a large group of men surrounded the wagon, stopping it. Without warning, the constable whipped the horses to high speed, breaking through the ring of troublemakers and racing off through the night.

The constable drove Joseph to the town of South Bainbridge, where he obtained a room for the two of them at an inn. To protect Joseph, he slept on the floor that night, a loaded gun at his side and his feet pressed against the door.

The next day, Joseph's trial began with a large crowd of people watching. His friend Joseph Knight found two good lawyers to defend him.

One of them, John Reid, had not wanted to take the case when Mr. Knight asked him to. He later confessed that a voice told him Joseph was innocent. Determined that justice would be done, he hurried as fast as he could to the place of the trial.

Joseph's enemies had also employed smart lawyers. They had combed the whole area for witnesses who would swear that Joseph had committed the crimes he'd been accused of. Although the trial went on all day, the judge was not convinced Joseph had done any wrong. The trial closed at midnight and Joseph was told he could go.

However, as soon as he was released, another constable came forward and arrested him. He was from Broome County, where Colesville was, and said that Joseph must stand trial there.

This constable began immediately to abuse and insult him. Because Joseph hadn't eaten since breakfast, he requested food.

"No," the constable said. "We do not have time."

He took Joseph fifteen miles away to a tavern where a number of men began to ridicule him. Pointing fingers and spitting on him, they said, "Why don't you prophesy for us, Joe?"

Joseph tried to ignore them. It was now afternoon, and since the tavern was not far from his home, Joseph asked permission to spend the evening with Emma. When the constable said no, he again asked for food. This time he was given some water and a bit of bread.

The next day Joseph faced a new trial. The same lawyers as before were there. The opposing lawyers tried their best to blacken Joseph's name, calling many witnesses to swear that he had done dreadful things. Joseph's lawyers followed. Telling his family about it later, Joseph said, "They spoke like men inspired of God, while those who were arrayed against me trembled under the sound of their voices."

Though the charges hurt Joseph, he sat quietly through the ordeal. As before, the charges against him were dismissed.

Mr. Reid was worried that Joseph would be harmed when he tried to leave.

Knowing the accusers were fond of liquor, Mr. Reid invited them into another room to drink so that Joseph could slip away unnoticed. As Joseph prepared to go, the constable who had arrested him walked up. "I want to apologize, Mr. Smith," he said. "I ask your forgiveness for my behavior toward you." He warned Joseph that a mob had sworn that if he was let go, they would tar and feather him and ride him out of town on a rail. Keeping an eye out for the mobbers, who were still busy drinking, the constable led him outside to safety through a private exit.

Joseph started off immediately to find Emma. He had not eaten anything except a little bread for almost two days, but he traveled without stopping because he did not want Emma to worry. At daybreak he arrived at the home of her sister. Emma was there, sick with anxiety about him. They both rejoiced at being together again.

A few days later, Joseph and Oliver Cowdery returned to Colesville to confirm the persons who had been baptized earlier. Not long after arriving, they saw a mob collecting to oppose them. Deciding it would be wise to leave, they hurried away.

CHAPTER 19

ON TO KIRTLAND AND BEYOND

Knowing that persecutions would very likely increase, Joseph longed for a place where the Saints could gather and worship as they pleased, as guaranteed by the Constitution of the United States.

In September, he sent several men westward on a mission. They had been called by revelation to preach to the Indian nations west of Missouri, people whose ancestors were spoken of in the Book of Mormon. Among these missionaries were Oliver Cowdery and Parley P. Pratt, a recent convert.

As they traveled, they sent back letters. They wrote of stopping near Kirtland, Geauga County, Ohio, where Parley had a good friend named Sidney Rigdon, a well-known preacher. Though doubtful at first, Sidney became so excited about the Book of Mormon that he was baptized and began preaching to everyone he knew. Soon many people joined the Church in the Kirtland area.

In December 1830, Sidney came to New York to visit Joseph, bringing along a friend, Edward Partridge, who also wanted to meet the Prophet. Joseph happily welcomed the two men, and it wasn't long before he baptized Edward. Joseph also received revelations from the Lord for both men, who each would contribute to the great work that was unfolding.

When Sidney heard about the persecution that plagued the Saints in New York, he urged Joseph to move on to Kirtland. Joseph prayed and received a revelation that the Church members should move to Ohio. Some were reluctant to obey. Joseph did his best to convince them that things would be better there, and eventually most agreed to go.

It was hard for Emma to face moving again. She had just recovered from a severe illness, and she was expecting another baby. The winter was cold, and Kirtland was at least 300 miles away. But she believed in her husband.

Before long, Joseph and Emma, along with Sidney and Edward, started off for Kirtland in a horse-drawn sleigh, traveling much of the way through deep snow. The other members of the Church would stay behind to sell their property and come as soon as they could. Joseph's group arrived in Kirtland in February 1831.

Emma sighed with relief when the sleigh finally came to a stop in front of the Newel K. Whitney store. The Whitneys were among the Kirtland Saints converted by Oliver and his fellow missionaries. They had never met Joseph but had prayed that he might come to Kirtland.

Joseph had seen them in vision praying, and when the sleigh stopped in front of the store, he jumped out, sprang up the stairs, and strode right up to where Brother Whitney was standing.

"Newel K. Whitney!" Joseph declared, putting out his hand, as if to an old friend. "Thou art the man!"

"You have the advantage of me," Newel replied to the stranger, shaking his hand mechanically. "I could not call you by name as you have me."

Joseph smiled. "I am Joseph the Prophet," he said. "You've prayed me here, now what do you want of me?"

Brother Whitney was pleased to meet Joseph, who introduced him to Emma. The Prophet and his wife had worried where they would live once they had arrived in Kirtland. They had come in obedience to the will of the Lord with faith that all would work out fine. Still, finding a good place to stay, especially in the dead of winter, could be very hard.

"You must stay at my home," Brother Whitney said. "We have a snug, warm house."

"Thank you," Emma whispered tiredly. "We will be happy to stay with you."

Gratefully, the Smiths moved in with the Whitney family. They later lived with the Morley family until a small frame home of their own could be built.

It was in this small house that Emma gave birth to twins on April 30, 1831. But the joy over their arrival turned to deep sorrow when both babies died within a few hours.

On the same day in a nearby village, a young mother named Julia Murdock died after having twins. Her husband, John, was a Church member who had three other small children to care for. Hearing of Joseph and Emma's loss, he came to ask if they would like to take the new babies.

"Oh, yes," Emma said weakly from her bed. "Bring them to me as soon as possible."

The twins came to the Smith home when they were nine days old. Emma called them Joseph and Julia and said they were her blessings from heaven.

As he faced the problems and blessings of his home life, Joseph continued to carry on the work of building and strengthening the Church. Moving to Kirtland gave him a chance to meet many of the new converts there and hear their stories. Among the converts was twelve-year-old Mary Elizabeth Rollins, who had been baptized with her mother in October 1830. After her baptism, John Whitmer had brought a copy of the Book of Mormon to Kirtland and left it with the presiding elder, Isaac Morley. At that time, it was the only copy in the whole area.

Mary Elizabeth, wanting very much to see the book, went to Brother Morley's house. Shyly she asked if she could look at it. Smiling at her eagerness, he put it into her hands. She held it for a moment and then asked him if she could take it home.

"I would like to read it," she explained.

"Well, young lady," Brother Morley said, "I've scarcely had time to look at it myself. And very few of the other brethren have even seen it."

Mary Elizabeth looked down at the book, then back up at him. "Brother Morley," she pleaded, "I must read this book."

He gazed at her for what seemed a long time. Then he said, "Child, if you will bring this book back before breakfast tomorrow morning, you may take it."

Mary Elizabeth clutched the book to her chest. "Oh, thank you," she said through her happy smile.

"Be very careful with it," he cautioned as she skipped away. "See that no harm comes to it."

That night and early the next morning, she read through much of the book, even memorizing the first part of it.

As promised, she returned the book to Brother Morley before breakfast. Since she'd had it for such a short time, he said, "I guess you did not read much in it."

She showed him how far she had read. His eyebrows went up.

"Well," he said, "I don't believe you can tell me one word of it."

Taking a deep breath, Mary Elizabeth began, "'I, Nephi, having been born of goodly parents, therefore I was taught somewhat in all the learning of my father.'" She went on to repeat the entire verse and tell Brother Morley about Nephi.

Brother Morley gazed at her in surprise. "Child," he said, "take this book home and finish it. I can wait."

Mary Elizabeth read the last page about the same time that Joseph arrived in Kirtland. When he came to visit the uncle with whom she lived, he noticed the book on the shelf.

"I sent that book to Brother Morley," Joseph said. "How did it get here?"

Mary Elizabeth's uncle told how she got it.

"Where is your niece?" Joseph asked him. She soon came into the room.

Joseph walked over and put his hands on her head, giving her a blessing. Then he gave her the book as a present. "I will give Brother Morley another one," he said.

Joseph was pleased to see the effect the Book of Mormon had on the Saints. He knew that as more people read the book, the Church would grow.

He was pleased, too, when Parley P. Pratt and other missionaries who had been sent westward returned to report. They had written to Joseph about their labors, but he was anxious to hear more.

"Tell me all about your mission," he directed Parley as they sat around a crackling fire.

"Well," Parley said, "there were some people who treated us badly, but others were eager to listen to us." He told Joseph of some of their experiences, then said, "I have a funny story to tell."

Joseph's eyes lit up. "Go ahead," he said. "I'm listening."

"It happened a few days after we left Kirtland," Parley said. He then went on to tell about being arrested one night while teaching someone about the Church. The charge was very minor, but the arresting officer insisted that Parley come along with him.

The policeman had taken him two miles away, where authorities waited to put him through a trial. It was clear to Parley that their real purpose was to stop his preaching. False witnesses swore against him.

When it was his turn to defend himself, he knew it would do no good to deny the charges, so he began to sing and preach to the assembled court.

"Stop that," the judge said. "Since you are obviously guilty, you must either pay a fine or go to prison."

"I guess it's prison then," Parley told him cheerfully, "because I have no money."

He was put in the custody of a policeman named Mr. Peabody, who took him to a nearby inn and locked him in his room. The next morning the other missionaries came by to see what they could do.

"Go on your way," Parley whispered to them. "I'll catch up with you."

They didn't want to leave him, but he insisted. After they left, Mr. Peabody took Parley downstairs to breakfast, then suggested they sit by the fire in the public room since it was quite cold. As soon as they were warm, Parley asked permission to go outside for some air. When the officer took him out, Parley said, "Mr. Peabody, are you good at a race?"

"Well, no, I'm not," Mr. Peabody said, who was much older than Parley. "But my big bulldog is. He has been trained to assist me in my duties, and he will take down any man at my bidding." He pointed at his dog, which sprawled nearby chewing on a bone. "His name is Stu-boy."

Parley didn't like the looks of the huge dog, but he said, "Mr. Peabody, you have given me an opportunity to preach, sing, and have also entertained me with lodging and breakfast. I must now go on my journey. If you are good at a race, you may accompany me. I thank you for all your kindness." Nodding politely, he said, "Good day, sir," and set off running as fast as he could.

Mr. Peabody was so shocked that for a moment he stood frozen in his tracks. By that time Parley was making his way through a field to a forest on the side of the road.

Behind him he heard Mr. Peabody clapping his hands and shouting to his dog. "Stu-boy," he hollered. "Take him, lay hold of him. I say, down with him."

Glancing over his shoulder as he ran, Parley saw Mr. Peabody pointing toward him. The huge bulldog had his eyes on Parley and was rumbling after him, snorting and growling. There was no way Parley could outrun the ferocious animal. He figured he was about to be chewed to bits.

Then he had an idea. Stopping suddenly, he clapped his hands as Mr. Peabody was doing and pointed in the direction of the forest. "Stu-boy," he hollered in imitation of Mr. Peabody. "Take him, lay hold of him."

The snarling dog sped off toward the forest.

Parley had veered to the side and was soon far away from both the officer and Stu-boy. Scarcely taking time to catch his breath, he hurried on to find his missionary companions. They had laughed with him when he told how he had played a trick on Mr. Peabody and his dog.

Joseph laughed, too, as Parley finished his story. "It reminds me of some of the adventures Oliver and I have had," he said. After chuckling about Stu-boy, he got back to business. "Tell me again about your visit to the Indian nations," Joseph said eagerly.

Parley nodded. "Well, as I wrote to you, we had to struggle through deep snow to get there, but we spoke with an important chief. After we'd talked to him for some time, he finally called other Indian leaders together. We taught them about the Book of Mormon and gave the chief a copy of the book. He told us through his interpreter that they were very grateful to their white friends who came so far to tell them of their forefathers. He said it made him glad here." Parley put a hand over his heart.

Joseph nodded approvingly. He gazed into the fire for a few moments, then said thoughtfully, "Think of it, Parley. Someday the gospel will be preached far beyond where you traveled. Someday the Church will spread throughout the whole earth."

CHAPTER 20

TAR AND FEATHERS

As the months went on, more Saints arrived from New York and Pennsylvania. Some people in Kirtland were impressed by the thrift and industry of the Church members. Others worried that the Saints with their twenty-five-year-old prophet would take over the town, and that some of the Church members would not be able to support themselves. The conversion of Sidney Rigdon and many others had caused an uproar in the area, and some people opposed their religious beliefs.

Joseph had received a revelation previously that Zion, a place for the Saints to gather and build a temple, would be "on the borders by the Lamanites." In June 1831, the Lord directed Joseph to go to Missouri with other Church leaders to hold a conference. While there he received another revelation, which made known to him that this was to be Zion and that a temple was to be built in a place called Independence in Jackson County.

After Joseph returned to Kirtland, he and Emma became the center of much of the social life of the Saints there. A constant stream of people came to their small house. Besides directing the affairs of the Church, Joseph had begun to put his revelations together in a book, and the frequent interruptions slowed his work. He and Emma were grateful when John and Elsa Johnson invited them to stay in their home thirty-six miles south of Kirtland. There they could enjoy more space and privacy to carry on their work.

While living at the Johnsons' home, Joseph continued working on an inspired translation of the Bible. Sidney Rigdon acted as scribe. One day they read a scripture suggesting that heaven must have more than one kingdom. As they pondered on this verse in a room with a dozen other men present, a vision opened up to Joseph and Sidney. It showed them that there were three degrees of glory in heaven.

The vision lasted over an hour, and when it ended, Sidney sat pale and limp. Smiling, Joseph remarked to others in the room, "Sidney is not used to it as I am." Throughout his life, Joseph would continue to receive revelations that blessed the growing Church.

But as the Church continued to grow, so did opposition.

In the early spring of 1832, the twins, little Joseph and Julia, came down with measles. They were very ill. Joseph and Emma soon became exhausted from caring for them. On the evening of March 24, Joseph told Emma that he would stay up and watch over little Joseph, the sickest of the babies, while she rested with Julia.

Wearily, Emma agreed. "I won't sleep for very long," she said. "Then it will be your turn."

In the middle of the night Emma came to tell Joseph to lie down on the trundle bed. Joseph rubbed a tired hand across his eyes. "All right," he said. Putting on his night clothes, he lay down and immediately fell asleep.

He hadn't slept very long when he was awakened by Emma's screams. Several men had rushed through the door. Groggy and confused, Joseph felt himself seized by rough hands before he could get to his feet. Some men carried him outside while others stayed back to hold the door closed so Emma and the Johnsons couldn't leave the house.

The cold night air brought Joseph fully awake. Young and strong, he fought back. When one large man named Warren Waste grabbed his foot, Joseph gave him a kick that sent him sprawling. That made the men even more angry.

"Hold still," snarled one of them, "or we'll kill you right here."

More men came to hold Joseph. Mr. Waste scrambled to his feet and thrust a blood-drenched hand in his face. "Just wait, I'll fix you," he snarled. Grabbing Joseph around the neck, he began choking him.

As Joseph lost consciousness, he heard Emma screaming for someone to come and help him.

The next thing he knew, he was stretched out on a plank, with most of his clothing torn off. He shivered with cold. Near his ear someone said, "Ain't we goin' to kill 'im?"

He expected them to do so. In the darkness he saw faces peering down at him. Strong hands still held his arms and legs. He couldn't move.

A voice said, "Simonds, Simonds, come here."

Joseph knew Simonds Ryder. He was one of the men holding him down. He seemed to be the leader of the mob.

Joseph appealed to him, saying, "Don't kill me, please. I have a family to care for."

Simonds growled some instructions to the other men. Then he walked a few steps away to hold council with those who had called him. Joseph could hear an occasional word and knew they were talking about whether or not to kill him. The decision was to let him live, but they were not ready to let him go. Instead, one man called him foul names and began to claw at him with his fingernails, leaving deep scratches on his body.

"Simonds, where's the tar bucket?" yelled one man. Another voice brayed, "Eli's left it behind."

There was the sound of running feet, and then Joseph smelled the stench of hot tar.

"Let's tar up his mouth," a voice rasped, and Joseph saw a thick paddle dripping with tar coming toward him. Joseph whipped his head around to keep the hot, smelly tar from choking him.

Then the neck of a small bottle was forced between his lips. Poison! He bit down hard, breaking a front tooth. He thought he must have broken the bottle, too, because the man holding it threw it on the ground, cursing.

Someone lifted the tar bucket, and Joseph felt the hot ooze spread over his naked body. He tried not to scream as the tar burned his skin and seeped into the bloody scratches. It was no use trying to kick himself free because several men sat on his legs.

"Call on that God of yours for help," a man bellowed just before splitting a pillow he carried and pouring the feathers from it onto the sticky tar.

Then suddenly the men were gone. Joseph raised himself onto an elbow, pulling tar from his lips so he could breathe easier. Painfully, he struggled to his feet and stumbled toward the lights of the house. He saw people running and thought for a moment that the men were coming back. Then he saw they were neighbors rushing to help.

Realizing how frightful he must look, Joseph called out for a blanket. Emma ran to the door, but when she saw Joseph she thought he was covered with blood. She fainted. While neighbor women attended to her, someone brought a blanket to cover Joseph before he staggered inside the house.

When Emma revived, she gasped at Joseph's awful condition, but then she quickly organized his friends to pull off the feathers and scrape the tar from his body. It took all night to clean him up. His skin was blistered and gashed. Emma and the others relieved the pain a little by rubbing lard into his wounds.

When morning came, he insisted on rising up and getting dressed.

"Joseph, you must rest," Emma admonished him.

He shook his head. "It's time for church," he said. "The Saints will be expecting me."

It was agonizing to put on his clothes, but he got dressed and went to preach to his congregation as if nothing had happened. Some of the mob were in the audience and heard Joseph speak about brotherly love and forgiveness.

During the morning, Joseph went to visit his friend and scribe, Sidney

Rigdon, who had also been beaten and tarred. Sidney was out of his mind and would not recover for some time.

Joseph's wounds healed, but baby Joseph, still weak from the measles, died a few days later. He was only eleven months old.

It had been a difficult time, but this was the worst blow of all. Joseph and Emma thought that things could not possibly get any worse.

CHAPTER 21

THE MARCH TO MISSOURI

Right after the terrible experiences of being tarred and feathered and losing his son, Joseph left for Missouri again, along with other Church leaders. Many of the Saints were gathering there in Jackson County, and Joseph wanted to see how they were getting along.

He found that life on the frontier was hard for the people. They had to work hard to provide for themselves. For the most part, however, they were cheerful and united. They were settling in and had even established the first newspaper in the area.

After his return to Kirtland, Joseph moved Emma and little Julia into the upstairs of Newel K. Whitney's store. In a corner bedroom there on November 6, 1832, Emma gave birth to a fine, healthy boy. Joseph and Emma named him Joseph Smith, after his father. Since they had lost four of their children earlier, they were happy and grateful to see their family now growing.

Two days after the baby was born, Joseph was chopping wood when three young men who had recently been converted came to visit him. One of them was Brigham Young, who said he'd read a copy of the Book of Mormon he'd received from a family member. Joseph shook hands with the men, put down his ax, and invited them to his home. He introduced them to Emma, who was in bed with baby Joseph.

The three men spent time with Joseph talking about the things of God. Joseph took an immediate liking to them and knew they would be valuable to the Church. That evening, Joseph confided to others that Brigham would someday lead the Church. For his part, Brigham would say of meeting Joseph, "He was all that any man could believe him to be, as a true Prophet."

Several weeks later, God gave Joseph a revelation called the Word of Wisdom, which was "a principle with a promise." The principle was that the Saints should not use liquor, tobacco, or hot drinks, meaning tea and coffee. Meat was to be eaten sparingly. The use of grain, fresh vegetables, and fruits was encouraged. The promise was that those who kept this commandment would receive health, wisdom, and knowledge and "shall run and not be weary, and shall walk and not faint."

A few months after this revelation, Joseph began receiving reports of terrible persecutions going on in Jackson County, Missouri. A mob had destroyed the newspaper printing office, and two men had been tarred and feathered. Other men were captured and brutally beaten. Frightened, some of the women and children had fled across the frozen prairie, leaving a trail of blood from their feet on the ground. Many of the Saints escaped across the Missouri River to Clay County, where they found temporary refuge.

The Church members pleaded with the legal authorities to help them stop these wrongs from happening. But in many cases, the local law men had taken part in the persecutions or at least had agreed to let them happen. They refused to help the Saints.

Finally, in February of 1834, the Church leaders in Missouri received a letter from the governor. It said that state officers would agree to help take them back to their homes. However, once there, it would be up to them to protect themselves.

That same month, back in Ohio, Joseph received a revelation that instructed him to call together a large group of men to march to Missouri and help the mistreated Saints. Messengers were sent out to recruit men. "Five hundred," the revelation had directed. If five hundred men could not be signed up, then three hundred. If not that many, then one hundred.

Eventually two groups were formed, totaling more than two hundred men. They called themselves Zion's Camp. Their purpose was to go to the aid of the people in Zion, the gathering place of the Saints in Missouri. One group was led by Joseph and the other by his brother Hyrum.

In early May, Joseph and his group, which included Brigham Young, started from Kirtland on their long march of hundreds of miles to Missouri. The area they traveled through was sparsely settled. Sometimes they were able to buy supplies so they could cook their own food. Other areas were practically wilderness, and they had to get along with very little food and water.

At the beginning of the march, the roads were so bad that the wagon wheels sank hub-deep in the mud. The men had to use ropes to help the horses pull the wagons along.

Whenever Joseph's group passed through a town, they attracted a lot of attention because it was strange for such a large number of men to travel together. People were curious and asked questions. Joseph told his men to say as little as possible. He did not want anyone to tell the mobs in Missouri that they were coming. So when they were questioned, the men said simply, "We are from the east and we are going to the west."

The closer Zion's Camp got to Missouri, the more opposition they faced. As they approached Indianapolis, they were told they would not be allowed to pass through the city. If necessary, force would be used to keep them out. Many of the men were worried, but Joseph told them they would get through without being hurt.

When they neared the city, he had as many men as possible get into the wagons, which he sent through at different times. He had those on foot go down several different streets in small groups.

They left the people in the city wondering when the big company they'd been watching for would be coming through.

Soon the marchers reached the open prairie, which was of great interest to them. Some of them had never before seen such large expanses of flat land. But now there was the problem of no springs of fresh water. Very often the only water they found was in swamps and was full of what they called "wigglers," little creatures that would grow into mosquitoes. They had to strain the water before drinking it.

When they came to a river, they were happy to have enough water. But they had to figure out how to cross it. Usually they just urged the horses into the stream. If it got deep, the horses swam, pulling the wagons along with them to the other side.

Sometimes they were able to use ferries.

As they traveled farther west, they found prairie rattlesnakes. When the men were about to kill the snakes, Joseph stopped them. "Let them alone," he said. "Don't hurt them. How will the serpent ever lose his venom if the servants of God possess the same disposition and continue to make war upon it?"

A few days later, when they stopped for a rest, Brother Humphreys, an older man, lay down to take a nap. When he awoke, he saw a large rattlesnake lying between him and his hat. Several men grabbed sticks. "It's a rattlesnake; let's kill it," one man said. But Brother Humphreys said, "No, I'll protect him. You shan't hurt him, for he and I had a good nap together."

As they drew close to Springfield, Illinois, Joseph sent a couple of men on ahead to see how people would treat them there. They returned saying the news of their approach had caused the local people to become excited, mostly from curiosity. A Church member who had settled there rode out to see them. He reported that Hyrum's group had passed on west the day before. "He has a fine company, and they all looked mighty pert," the man said.

On Sunday, June 1, Zion's Camp had a preaching service just outside of Springfield. Many local people joined them, suspecting they were the Mormon group they'd heard about. Joseph and the other leaders decided to confuse them. They asked several men who had once been preachers for other churches to deliver the sermons. When the Springfield citizens asked who they were, they truthfully identified themselves as having been a Baptist preacher, a Campbellite, a Reformed Methodist, and a Restorationer. The citizens listened to the sermons. Then they left, wondering what had happened to the Mormons.

The closer the small army got to Missouri, the more rumors they heard about an enemy force being sent to drive them back. Some men in Zion's Camp began to murmur and grumble. They complained not only about the coming opposition but also about the miserable conditions they were forced to endure. Joseph told them that if they would be faithful, they would get along all right.

By the time the group reached the banks of the Mississippi River, one man had come down with mumps and another with fever. Others were lame, and all were tired. Complaints were increasing.

When the sick men were well enough to march again, they crossed the mighty Mississippi by ferry. They camped for a while in a pleasant grove near a spring of fresh water at a place called Salt River. On Sunday, June 8, Hyrum's group of volunteers joined them. Over the next few days they went through military drills, preparing themselves for whatever they would face when they got to Jackson County.

Joseph sent two men to see if the governor of Missouri was ready to fulfill his promise to help the Saints return to their homes. They came back to report that the governor refused. He had decided not to send troops to help the Saints reclaim their own lands.

So after traveling hundreds of miles and suffering from hunger, thirst, fatigue, and lack of sleep, the members of Zion's Camp faced the disappointment of no support from state leaders. The only thing to do was to keep going and join the Saints who had fled from Jackson County into Clay County. Reports reached them that the mobs were swelling in numbers to oppose them, even though good people were telling them to let the Mormons alone.

News came that a mob of more than two hundred men had set out with designs to "kill Joe Smith and his army." But a ferocious storm came up that forced the mobbers to crawl under their wagons or into hollow trees to save their lives from the huge hailstones that fell. After the storm was over, their

After all of the other difficulties, many of the men were struck down by cholera.

ammunition was so soaked that they had to return to their homes without fighting.

Joseph and his group, who had sheltered in an old meetinghouse, were unharmed.

In the end, Zion's Camp was unable to help the Saints of Jackson County, Missouri, return to their homes. After all of the other difficulties they had overcome, many of the men were struck down by cholera, becoming seriously ill. Some died.

The Lord gave a revelation through Joseph Smith in which He told the Church members they "should wait for a little season for the redemption of Zion." Before that would happen, He said, the Saints would first complete the temple they had already begun building in Kirtland. To the obedient, the Lord promised, "I have prepared a blessing and an endowment for them, if they continue faithful." He said that they were "brought thus far for a trial of their faith."

Following this revelation, Zion's Camp was disbanded, and most of its members returned to Kirtland. Some of the Saints murmured, saying they considered the march a failure.

Yet many benefits came from Zion's Camp. Those who were faithful to the Church and loyal to Joseph were strengthened and united. Many of the Church's most important leaders would be chosen from the Zion's Camp group. They were men who had been tested by trials and found worthy.

Brigham Young and others in Zion's Camp also learned important skills about making long and difficult journeys involving hundreds of people with their wagons, animals, supplies, and belongings. When he spoke of it later, Brigham said, "I would not exchange the experience gained in that expedition for all the wealth of Geauga County."

CHAPTER 22

BUILDING A TEMPLE

Before Joseph left on the Zion's Camp march to Missouri, he'd had a revelation that the Saints should build a temple in Kirtland. It was to be a large and beautiful structure, the first building of its kind since the temple in Jerusalem where Jesus preached. Joseph, Sidney Rigdon, and Frederick G. Williams saw in vision what the temple would look like. But how were they to build it? The members of the Church in Kirtland were very poor.

Most of the Saints did not fully understand what this temple was to be. Up until now they had been meeting in a log house or other buildings too small to hold all the new converts who were coming in. "Can't we just build a bigger log house?" the brethren asked one day in June 1833 when they met to talk about it. "We might be able to afford that." Others suggested something more elaborate.

Joseph shook his head at the idea of logs. "We're not building a house for man, but for God," he said. "Shall we, brethren, build a house for our God, of logs?"

"What matters is what's in our hearts," they said. "Can't we worship just as well in a house of logs?"

"No," Joseph said. "We must give the Lord our very best. We have been commanded to establish a house of prayer, a house of fasting, a house of faith, a house of learning, a house of glory, a house of order, a house of God." He paused and gazed at the assembled brethren. "I have a better plan than building a house of logs. I have a plan of the house of the Lord given by God Himself, and you will soon see by this the difference between our calculations and His idea of things."

He explained to them the pattern as it had been revealed to him. The temple would be a fine two-story building with room inside for hundreds of people. The lower floor would be a meetinghouse and the upper level a school. Large windows on each floor would let in light. A tall steeple would top the building.

The brethren were delighted with the plans Joseph showed them. "But how can we do this?" they asked. "We're struggling just to live day by day."

"It will require sacrifices from all of us," Joseph admitted. "But we can do it. Let's go right now and select a spot to build it."

He led them to a large field that he and his brothers had sown with wheat the previous fall. Together the men chose a location in the northwest corner of the field. Within a few minutes they had removed a fence and leveled the standing wheat stalks. Hyrum Smith immediately began digging a trench for a wall.

This was on a Saturday. On Monday they came back to continue what they had started. They split their time between the work they did for a living and their labor on the temple.

The cornerstone was laid on July 23, 1833. It was time to start on the walls. This would require a great deal of money. Joseph urged the Saints to contribute all they could.

The walls of the temple were only partially finished when the men left in May 1834 to participate in the Zion's Camp march. While they were gone, the women labored to make stockings, trousers, and jackets so that when the men came back they would have the right kind of clothes to work in.

When they got back, the men returned to building the temple with greater energy, inspired by the revelation Joseph received in Missouri. One of the big work projects for the men was to carve out large pieces of stone from a nearby quarry and bring them to the temple site. Joseph, who enjoyed working with his hands, joined in the quarrying, toiling right along with the rest of the men.

Every Saturday many of the men took their wagons and teams of horses to the quarry to carry the stones where they were needed. Others put the stones together, and the walls of the temple rose. When the outside coating was being added to the sandstone walls, dishes and glassware were gathered to be crushed and worked into the plaster to make it sparkle.

To the Saints, the temple became more than a meetinghouse and a school. It was a visible symbol of the Kingdom of God.

During all of this building activity, the Saints had to protect the temple from those who wanted to destroy what they had built. Some of the men were chosen to sleep during the day so they could stand watch at night. Even those who worked on the building during the day kept weapons nearby to drive away anybody who might come to tear down the walls. At night they slept in their working clothes with guns close by.

In 1835, enemies arose within the Church. They charged Joseph with doing things wrong. The walls of the temple were only partly built at the time, and the Saints sometimes used a nearby schoolhouse for meetings. During one meeting in the school, the Saints saw tears trickling down Joseph's face.

After the opening song, Joseph knelt in prayer, his back to the audience to hide his tears. One man later said he had never heard such a simple but powerful prayer. He said Joseph talked to God "as though He was present listening as a kind father would to a child." Joseph prayed for "those who accused him of having gone astray." When he finished, he rose from his knees to preach a sermon.

The next week, his accusers apologized.

During his days in Kirtland, Joseph encouraged the starting of schools, not only to educate children but also to instruct adults and prepare missionaries to be sent out. He even started a class in Hebrew, taught by a Jewish professor, for

To the Saints, the temple was a visible symbol of the Kingdom of God.

people who wanted to study the Old Testament in the original Hebrew language.

Finally, the temple was completed and ready to be dedicated. The poverty-stricken Saints had sacrificed much to build it, donating every penny they could spare.

On the morning of the dedication ceremony, March 27, 1836, a large crowd gathered outside the temple. At eight o'clock when the doors at last swung open, eight hundred people crowded inside. They found seats on the benches that occupied the center of the main hall. Church leaders sat behind the pulpits at each end of the hall, and members of the choir sat in each of the four corners.

Ushers closed the doors after every seat was filled. But there were still many people outside, faithful Saints who had sacrificed time and money to help build the temple. Joseph had them go to a nearby schoolhouse and hold a meeting, but not everyone could fit in that hall either. So Joseph asked that the whole ceremony be repeated four days later to give everyone a chance to attend.

At 9:00 A.M. the solemn assembly began with songs and a prayer. Sidney Rigdon, one of Joseph's counselors, spoke and later asked the people to sustain Joseph as a prophet. After more singing and a break, Joseph spoke briefly and presented other Church officers for a sustaining vote. "I promise you," he said, "that if you uphold these men in their stations, the blessings of heaven will be yours."

After another song, Joseph stood and gave the dedicatory prayer he had received through revelation. In it he asked the Lord to accept the temple which He had commanded to be built. The ceremony went on for some time and included the choir singing "The Spirit of God Like a Fire Is Burning," a song written for the dedication. As part of the meeting, the congregation gave the Hosanna Shout, something that is still done today each time a temple is dedicated.

Some people saw angels there in the temple. Others experienced spiritual gifts, such as speaking in tongues, prophecy, revelation, and visions. Many people felt the Spirit deeply and would remember the dedication their whole lives.

On the next Sunday, April 3, Joseph and Oliver Cowdery knelt in prayer in the temple. As they did so, the Lord Himself appeared. According to the record made of this vision, "His eyes were as a flame of fire," His hair "white like the pure snow," and His voice "as the sound of the rushing of great waters."

Speaking of the temple for which the Saints had sacrificed so much, He declared, "I have accepted this house." Then Moses, Elias, and Elijah appeared one at a time to give Joseph and Oliver the keys, or special authority, that were needed to do such things as missionary and temple work. The main purpose for building the Kirtland Temple was to make it possible to receive these keys.

It was a time of great rejoicing for the Kirtland Saints. They had worked hard and sacrificed much for the time when their shining temple would be completed. But this time of peace and happiness would not last long.

CHAPTER 23

TRIALS OF FAITH

The Saints had sacrificed greatly to build the Kirtland Temple, and after it was finished, they faced even greater financial hardships. As more and more people moved to the Kirtland area, the price of land rose higher and higher. It was expensive for people just to live.

Joseph and the other Saints borrowed money for building projects and to help their families get by. They wanted to start a bank, but the local government would not let them. Instead, they formed the Kirtland Safety Society, which worked like a bank but eventually failed, which meant people lost most of the money they had put in it.

Across the country, other banks began to fail. People had little money. Some of the Saints grew very unhappy. They blamed their problems on Joseph and other Church leaders.

In September 1837, Joseph and Sidney Rigdon left for Missouri, and while they were gone, some of the Church members rebelled and turned away from the Prophet. Others, like Brigham Young, stood up for Joseph. Before long, the rebellious people began to persecute Brigham, and in December, he had to flee Kirtland to save his life.

After Joseph and Sidney returned, Joseph tried to get the rebels to repent, but the opposition was too great. Some people threatened him, and he felt it was unsafe for him to stay in Kirtland. He decided to move to Far West, Missouri, a town settled by the Saints.

One night he held a council of Church leaders to make plans. At the end of the meeting he said, "Well, brethren, one thing is certain. I shall see you again, no matter what happens. For I have a promise of life for five years, and they cannot kill me until that time has expired."

Later that evening, he had the feeling he should leave Kirtland immediately. He and his family gathered together just enough bedding and clothing to get by. They left in the dead of night on January 12, 1838.

Joseph took his family to the home of some friends, where he thought they would be safe from the men he knew were pursuing him. They would gather more supplies, and then make the rest of the journey by covered wagon.

Joseph and Sidney continued on horseback. They rode all night, traveling to Norton, Ohio, where they arrived early in the morning. The Saints there sheltered them until their families caught up thirty-six hours later. After they were rested, they all pushed on toward Far West.

When they reached Dublin, Indiana, they found Brigham Young and other Church members there. By that time, Joseph and his family were out of money and could travel no farther. After trying to get a job cutting and sawing wood, Joseph went to Brigham and said he would now have to depend on him. "I look to you for counsel in this case," he said.

Brigham did not think he really meant what he was saying. When Joseph insisted he did mean it, Brigham said, "If you will take my counsel, it will be that you rest yourself and be assured that you shall have money in plenty to pursue your journey."

Joseph did as he said. In the meantime, a man came to ask Brigham's advice about some property he had been trying to sell. Brigham told him what to do. In three days the man came back to say he had a good offer. He was so grateful that he gave Brigham three hundred dollars. Brigham gave the money to Joseph so he and his family could continue their journey.

Soon they and others were on their way again, traveling through Indiana and Illinois and crossing the Mississippi River by ferry at Quincy, Illinois. Now they were in Missouri. But there was still a long way to go.

Finally, two months and one day from the time they left Kirtland, Joseph and his companions arrived in Far West. As they approached, they were met by a group of Church members who came to escort them safely to the end of their journey. They were welcomed in Far West with open arms and warm hearts.

The people were happy to have Joseph in their midst and flocked to listen to him speak. Many came out of pure curiosity because they had heard so much about him. Some wondered why he had left Kirtland. Seated outdoors on a wagon box, Joseph spoke to a crowd that gathered. It included old settlers who did not belong to the Church.

"You have heard many reports about me," Joseph began. "Some perhaps are true and others not true. I know what I have done and I know what I have not done."

He went on to testify, "The Book of Mormon is true, just what it purports to be, and for this testimony I expect to give an account in the day of judgment." Joseph seemed to sense the problems that were ahead, because he also said, "If I obtain the glory which I have in view I expect to wade through much tribulation." As he brought his speech to a close, he said, "The Savior declared the time was coming when secret or hidden things should be revealed on the housetops. Well, I have revealed to you a few things, if not on the house top, on the wagon top."

To the Church leaders back in Kirtland, Joseph wrote, "Dear Brethren, You may be assured that so friendly a meeting and reception paid us well for our long seven years of servitude, persecution, and affliction in the midst of our enemies, in the land of Kirtland." He went on to say, "The Saints at this time are in union, and peace and love prevail throughout." He reassured them, "We have no uneasiness about the power of our enemies in this place to do us harm."

During this peaceful period, Joseph found time to both work and play. He spent time studying and working with his hands. When he tired of study, he would play games with children around the house, and then go back to studying again.

One day he was playing a game of ball with a group of young boys. Eventually, the boys got tired of playing. Joseph called them together and said, "Let's build a log cabin." Their enthusiasm revived, the boys went off with him to build a cabin for a widow.

The peace that Joseph and the Saints enjoyed, however, did not last long. There were many people in the surrounding areas who were afraid of the Saints. Among other things, they thought the Mormons would take over and elect only their own people to public office. When it was time for an election, the brethren went to the polling place to vote, which was their right. But a mob had formed to prevent them from doing so.

As the Saints waited to vote, one of the mob began picking on a Mormon much smaller than he was. The man backed away, but the bully jumped on him, savagely beating him. Another Mormon tried to pull the bully off, but other members of the mob attacked him, too. A husky Saint, grabbing a piece of wood to use as a weapon, began striking back. Other Church members joined in, and the mob, surprised by how hard the Saints defended their rights, soon backed off.

That night some of the mob wrote letters to all the towns in the area, begging for assistance to fight the Mormons. They claimed that Joseph Smith himself had killed seven men on election day. They also said that he planned to draw all of his people together and murder those who were not members of his church.

It was all lies. No one had died in the fight, and Joseph had not even been at the polls when it occurred. But his enemies believed the rumors and accepted them as truth. Soon those who opposed the Church began organizing to drive out the Saints, just as they had done in Jackson County and elsewhere.

For years, the Saints had suffered illegal persecution from those who did not like their way of life. This time, however, would be different. This time, the Saints would fight for their rights as American citizens to settle where they wished. After years of patient suffering, they decided they had been driven long enough.

CHAPTER 24

MORE MOBS

The Church members' efforts to defend their rights proved hopeless. Mobs formed and harassed the Saints, driving them from their homes and severely beating some men. Joseph and other Church members went to Daviess County to see what they could do. They searched for weapons and destroyed what they thought were mob centers. They hoped their strong response would discourage further attacks.

But their actions just gave their enemies more reasons to turn people against the Saints. In the course of the Mormon War, as it was called, some people on both sides broke the law. Those who controlled the government seemed to ignore it when the anti-Mormons did things wrong. The Saints' mistakes, however, were counted against them.

In a battle near Crooked River in Ray County, one group of Saints tried to rescue some others who had been captured. One Missourian and three Mormons died, and several were wounded on both sides.

One-sided reports of this battle and other conflicts were given to Missouri governor Lilburn W. Boggs. Not bothering to investigate and learn the facts, he issued an order. "The Mormons must be treated as enemies," he declared.

"They must be exterminated or driven from the state, if necessary, for the public good. Their outrages are beyond all description."

Three days after the order went out, more than two hundred Missourians attacked the small Mormon settlement of Haun's Mill. These Missourians had not yet seen the governor's order, but they began killing people anyway. The Saints tried their best to defend themselves, but they were badly outnumbered. The Missourians killed seventeen men and boys and wounded fourteen other Saints.

Even before this outrage, many of the Saints in outlying areas had moved into Far West. But thousands of militia soldiers soon appeared, sent by the governor supposedly to keep the peace.

Some of them seemed anxious to exterminate or drive out the Saints. The Church members were surrounded and badly outnumbered. Joseph and other

Church leaders were unwilling to fight lawful militia sent by the governor. Instead, they agreed to meet with the militia leaders, hoping to settle the problem and preserve the lives of the Saints. To their surprise, they were taken prisoner by the soldiers.

Parley P. Pratt later described the scene, saying, "The haughty general rode up, and, without speaking to us, instantly ordered his guard to surround us. They did so very abruptly, and we were marched into camp surrounded by thousands of savage looking beings. These all set up a constant yell, like so many bloodhounds let loose upon their prey."

So loud was their noise that the Saints in Far West heard it. Joseph's parents came to the door of their home to listen. When they heard gunshots, they thought Joseph was being murdered. His father cried out, "My God, my God, they have killed my son."

Mother Lucy, her heart breaking, had to help him to his bed because he did not have the strength to stand on his feet. They huddled there, listening to the shrieking of the militia.

Joseph and his companions had not been shot but were being harassed and threatened. They were treated with contempt and made to lie on the ground in the rain that night, without any shelter. They were forced to listen to their guards tell about bashing one Mormon's brains out. "With his own rifle," a soldier boasted.

The next day, some of the soldiers went around raiding the homes of the Saints. They were supposed to be searching for guns, but some of the rougher men used the search as an excuse to abuse the Saints. Not all of the militia men were bad. Some did their best to protect the citizens from harm.

About noon on that day, soldiers reached Hyrum's house, where he was lying sick. They took him and one other man prisoner, forcing them to the militia camp at gunpoint, making seven prisoners in all. That night, the militia officers held a meeting in which Joseph and the other prisoners were sentenced to be shot the next morning in the Far West public square.

But one of the high officers, Brigadier-General Alexander Doniphan, objected. "It is cold blooded murder," he said, "and I wash my hands of it." He threatened to withdraw his entire brigade and march them away if the terrible sentence were carried out.

The commanding general then changed his mind, saying that Joseph and the others would just be held as prisoners. They would be hauled by the militia to Jackson County, where they would be tried in a court of law.

When Joseph learned what was happening, he demanded to see the commanding general. "Why are we treated this way?" he asked. "We have not done anything worthy of such treatment. We have always supported the Constitution and democracy."

"I know it," the general answered with a sneer, "and that is the reason why I want to kill you, or have you killed."

Joseph could do nothing more.

The next morning, before the start of the sixty-mile journey to Jackson County, Joseph, Hyrum, and their friends were allowed to go briefly to their homes to get fresh clothes. But they were forbidden to speak to their families.

When Joseph entered his house, Emma and the children threw themselves upon him, their eyes streaming with tears. They thought he had been shot during the night and rejoiced that he was still alive. They dreaded having him dragged away to prison or worse.

He had time only to change his clothes and offer a quiet, fervent prayer for the safety of his loved ones before the soldiers forced his family away.

As Joseph and the other prisoners were led off, they worried about their families. As far as they knew, they might never see them again.

CHAPTER 25

PRISONERS

As the prisoners were being loaded into wagons for the trip to Jackson County, Joseph's parents were alarmed to see a man dashing toward their house. "If you want to see your sons alive one more time," the messenger gasped to Mother Lucy, "you must go immediately, before they start off for Independence."

Mother Lucy, a sick Father Joseph, and their youngest daughter, Lucy, started at once for the wagons. They found a noisy crowd surrounding the wagon where Joseph and Hyrum were held. They could not get close to it. Mother Lucy drew herself up. "I am the mother of the Prophet," she declared to those around her. "Is there not a gentleman here who will assist me to that wagon, that I may take a last look at my children and speak to them once more before I die?"

Most of the men nearby shouted and jeered at her, but one man came forward. "I'll help you," he said kindly.

Shouldering a path through the crowd, he led Mother Lucy and Lucy to the wagon. Curses and threats filled their ears as they looked with dismay at the strong cloth cover nailed across the wagon. "Hyrum," the man called, "your mother and sister are here."

A hand came through a small opening between the nails holding the cover down. Mother Lucy grasped it and leaned down to whisper to Hyrum.

"No talking!" someone growled. "Move along, move along."

Swiftly kissing Hyrum's hand, Mother Lucy moved to the back part of the wagon. "Joseph," she said softly.

Joseph thrust his hand out.

"No talking," the harsh voice repeated.

Defiantly Mother Lucy leaned closer. "Joseph," she said, her voice quavering. "Do speak to your poor mother once more. I cannot bear to go until I hear your voice."

"God bless you, Mother," Joseph cried from under the heavy cover.

There was a shout and the crack of a whip. The horses hitched to the wagon leaped forward, just as Joseph's sister leaned down to press her lips to his hand.

Mother Lucy and Lucy could do nothing but sob with despair as the wagon was jerked away from them.

Several brethren struggled to get close enough to shake hands with Joseph, but the mob drove them back. Joseph was able to raise the wagon cover just a little so he could reach toward them. "Good-bye," he called and was soon out of sight.

The militia men and their captives traveled twelve miles before camping that night near Crooked River. Joseph and Hyrum and the other prisoners were allowed to get out of the wagons to eat and walk about. General Wilson, the commander of the militia, became quite sociable as they sat around the campfires. He spoke freely about the murders and robberies that had been committed against the Mormons in Missouri.

"We knew perfectly well that from the beginning the Mormons have not been the aggressors at all," he told the captives. "You were crowded to the last extreme and compelled to self-defense," he said, "and this has been construed into treason, murder, and plunder."

He went on to say that these actions in self-defense gave the law authorities reason not to protect them. He seemed amused by the whole thing.

But as he spoke with the prisoners, his manner seemed to soften. He told them that some of the troops wanted to hang them on the first tree they saw, but he would not let anyone hurt them. "We just intend to exhibit you in Independence, to let the people see what a set of fine fellows you are." Then he added, "And we intend to keep you from General Clark and his troops who are so stuffed with lies and prejudice that they would shoot you down in a moment."

This left the group wondering. Was General Wilson truly interested in their safety? Or did he just want the honor of being the one to bring in the captives for display in Independence?

Joseph had a revelation that night. The next morning, as the militia march began again, he told the other prisoners about it. "Be of good cheer, brethren," he said softly so the soldiers could not hear. "The word of the Lord came to me last night that our lives should be given us, and that whatever we may suffer during this captivity, not one of our lives should be taken." They were all greatly comforted by this knowledge.

When they reached the banks of the Missouri River across from Jackson County, the militia brigade halted for a few hours. The prisoners were taken to an inn where they could shave, change their clothes, and have something to eat. Then a message came that General Clark and his troops were close behind and wanted the prisoners to be turned over to him.

Not knowing that the governor had made General Clark his superior officer, General Wilson was not about to give up Joseph and the others. He urged part of his brigade onward with the prisoners, leaving the rest of his troops behind to follow the next morning. They crossed the river by ferry, marched about a mile, and camped for the night.

The next morning Joseph took the opportunity to preach the gospel to some curious people who came by to see the prisoners. One lady was so touched by what he said that she went away crying and praying aloud that the Lord would take care of Joseph and the other brethren.

On this day's march, the group came upon a number of settlements. Word had gone on ahead that Joseph Smith and other Mormon leaders were coming. Hundreds of people turned out to get a glimpse of the prisoners. General Wilson marched his men along like a parade, with Joseph, Hyrum, and the other men riding in carriages so the crowds could see them. Sometimes the general halted the parade so he could point out each captive by name.

Some of the people were hostile, but most were simply curious. Some expressed compassion and sympathy to Joseph and his friends. Some wanted to converse and ask questions. Joseph and the other prisoners took these opportunities to shake hands and tell about their beliefs.

By the time they reached Independence, a cold rain was pouring down. But still hundreds of people crowded around to witness the progress of the militia and wagons. General Wilson even called for bugles to sound triumphant blasts to announce their coming.

Eventually the troops were dismissed. The prisoners were taken into a comfortable house with a warm fire blazing in the fireplace. After the men cleaned up, they were led to an inn where they were fed well. Back at the house, they were given paper and pens and candles so they could write to their families.

Joseph wrote a letter to Emma. In it he said, "I would inform you that I am well, and we are all in good spirits as regards our own fate. We have been protected by the Jackson County boys in the most genteel manner, and arrived here in the midst of a splendid parade. Instead of going to jail, we have a good house provided for us and the kindest treatment. I have great anxiety about you and my lovely children. If we are permitted to stay any time here, we have obtained a promise that we may have our families brought to us."

He described the conflict between General Wilson and General Clark over the fate of the prisoners. "I do not know where it will end," he said.

Despite their uneasiness about what would happen to them, Joseph and his friends enjoyed the kind treatment that was given to them in Independence. They were even invited to dine one evening with General Wilson. Even so, they were still prisoners and kept apart from their families.

Eventually they received bad news. General Clark had won out in his demands to take control of the captives. They would be carried on to Richmond, which was the headquarters of General Clark and his army of about four thousand men.

General Wilson, who now knew that General Clark was his superior and had to be obeyed, insisted on providing several armed officers to go along to protect the prisoners. These guards were friendly. When they got drunk at night and lay down to sleep, they gave Joseph and his party their pistols to use in case anybody came by to bother them.

Just before the group reached Richmond, they were met and surrounded by a company of General Clark's troops. The soldiers, with weapons displayed, marched the prisoners into the city, where again they had to endure being exhibited to hundreds of curious citizens.

Before Joseph and the six prisoners with him arrived in Richmond, forty-six other Latter-day Saint prisoners had already been brought there and put in the county courthouse, which was not yet finished and open to the cold. When Joseph's group arrived, they were put into an old house and forced to sleep on the cold floor. Since the log house was not really secure, Joseph and his companions were chained together. Men with guns guarded them, ready to shoot them if they tried to escape.

As bad as the physical situation was, the spiritual and emotional conditions were even more miserable. The guards were rowdy and foulmouthed. They enjoyed seeing how their filthy language and vulgar stories offended the prisoners. They delighted in telling how they had defiled Mormon women and shot or beaten men, women, and children.

For several days the captives endured these conditions while they waited to see what would happen to them. Very early one morning after the guards had told particularly vile stories throughout the dark, cold hours of the night, Joseph suddenly rose to his feet. His chains jangled as he spoke in a voice of thunder.

"SILENCE, ye fiends of the infernal pit," he roared. "In the name of Jesus

Christ I rebuke you and command you to be still; I will not live another minute and hear such language. Cease such talk, or you or I die THIS INSTANT!"

Standing there in terrible dignity, he stared at the guards until they crouched at his feet, begging his pardon. Then, lowering their weapons, they crept into a corner where they stayed until time for a change of guards.

Parley P. Pratt later wrote that he had seen English law courts and the American Congress and had tried to imagine kings and royalty. "But dignity and majesty have I seen but once," he said, "as it stood in chains, at midnight, in a dungeon in an obscure village of Missouri."

CHAPTER 26

ESCAPE

After several days in their cold, dreary prison, Joseph and the other brethren still did not know what was going to happen to them. They had not yet been formally charged with any crimes. Nobody could give them a satisfactory explanation as to why they were being held by the military since they were not military prisoners, merely ministers of the gospel.

Joseph wrote a letter to Emma saying, "I think that the authorities will discover our innocence and set us free. But if this blessing cannot be obtained, I have this consolation, that I am an innocent man."

He went on to say, "Tell the children that I am alive and trust I shall come and see them before long. Comfort their hearts all you can and try to be comforted yourself." His children now included two more boys, Frederick and Alexander.

Eventually the men were granted a hearing before a judge. The judge refused to hear anything about the terrible crimes the Missourians had committed against the Saints. He wanted to listen only to the things the Saints had done wrong. Among other things, people argued that because Joseph and the others believed what the Bible said about God's kingdom spreading through the earth, they were guilty of treason, or betraying the government.

According to the law, the prisoners had the right to present witnesses to testify in their defense, too. But before any of the witnesses could testify, they were thrown into prison or scared away by threats from the mobs.

The judge became exasperated. He told the prisoners, "If you have any witnesses, bring them forward. The Court cannot delay forever. It has waited several days already."

At that moment a member of the Church by the name of Mr. Allen was seen passing the window of the courtroom. Joseph asked that he might be sworn in as a witness for them, and the judge agreed. Mr. Allen began to give his testimony about the innocence of the prisoners, telling about the murders and robberies committed by their accusers. But because he was a Church member, he was interrupted by cries of, "Kick him out!" "Shoot him!" "Kill him."

The judge ordered Mr. Allen out of the court. After the guard threw him out, the yelling mob outside closed in on him, and he barely escaped with his life.

The lawyer helping Joseph and the brethren finally told them it was no use to say anything in their defense. "Though a legion of angels from the opening heavens should declare your innocence," he said, "the court and the people have decreed your destruction."

The court finally decided to release most of the prisoners. But some of the leaders, including Joseph, Hyrum, and Sidney Rigdon, were held for a later trial. They were to be taken to Liberty, Missouri, where they would be thrown into the Clay County jail.

The next morning, a wagon pulled in front of the door of the log house where Joseph and his friends were kept. A blacksmith came inside to handcuff the prisoners and chain them together. "The judge plans to keep you locked up until all the Mormons have been driven out of Missouri," the blacksmith said as he adjusted their chains. "He says there's no law for Mormons in this state." Finishing, the blacksmith looked up at the chained men. Peering into their faces, he said grimly, "He swore he will see you exterminated, as the Governor ordered."

The prisoners were led out of the house and ordered to get into the wagon. As they traveled along the road, they were once more exhibited to the people who lived there.

Their destination, the Liberty Jail, was a two-story building with walls of rough stones. Inside the stone wall was a second wall of squared oak logs. A space twelve inches wide between the two walls was filled with rocks. If the prisoners tried to dig through the log wall, the loose rocks would fall down to fill up the space. It was a very strong jail.

The lower room of the building was a dungeon, lighted by small openings with heavy iron bars across the windows. It was damp and drafty, and the men were given very few blankets to keep out the winter cold. They would be kept there for four months and five days.

"Do not think that our hearts faint as though some strange thing had happened unto us," Joseph wrote to the Church members. "We have seen and been assured of all these things beforehand and have an assurance of a better hope than that of our persecutors. Therefore God has made our shoulders broad that we can bear it."

Some of the guards in the Liberty Jail delighted in taunting and humiliating the prisoners. At times the food they gave Joseph and the other prisoners made them ill.

Emma was able to come from Far West and visit Joseph three times during this ordeal. He advised her that the family should gather up what belongings they could and move on to Illinois. They did so, traveling through great hardships. On March 7, 1839, Emma wrote from Illinois to Joseph, saying, "I shall not attempt to write my feelings altogether." Instead, she wrote about the children, saying, "We are all well at present, except Frederick, who is quite sick. Little Alexander, who is now in my arms, is one of the finest little fellows you ever saw in your life. He is so strong that with the assistance of a chair he will run all around the room."

"The people in this state are very kind indeed," she wrote. "They are doing much more than we ever anticipated they would." She ended by saying, "I hope there are better days to come to us yet."

Despite Emma's hopes for better days, life in the jail caused Joseph and his friends to feel discouraged at times. Joseph finally cried to the Lord, asking to know how long the Saints would continue to suffer. The Lord answered, "My son, peace be unto thy soul." He told Joseph his troubles would be "but a small moment." "And then," He promised, "if thou endure it well, God shall exalt thee on high; thou shalt triumph over all thy foes." The Lord taught Joseph that all his trials and problems would give him experience, and be for his good.

The revelation brought comfort to Joseph and his fellow prisoners. At the same time, they were becoming less and less hopeful of receiving justice in the Missouri courts. Sidney Rigdon had been very ill ever since the men had been chained on the cold floor in Richmond. The guards both there and in the Liberty Jail refused to do anything for him.

After Joseph and the others petitioned several times for some kind of relief, Sidney was allowed to leave. "He will have to go in the night, unknown to any of the citizens or they will kill him," the judge said. Sidney was released and, despite his sickness, made it safely to Illinois.

As for the rest of the prisoners, the judge said people would object and turn their hatred toward him if he let them go. "If I did," he told them, "I would fear for my own life as well as yours." He was sorry they had to be locked up when they were innocent. "The people know you are innocent," he said, "but they fear that you will become too numerous." He revealed that there were men riding into town every day, stirring up the minds of the people against them. They would surely be killed if they were released from jail.

As time went on, things seemed to change a little. Joseph wrote to the Church members, saying, "As nigh as we can learn, the public mind has been for a long time turning in our favor and the majority is now friendly. Public opinion is beginning to look with feelings of indignation against our oppressors and to say that the Mormons were not in the fault in the least. We think that truth, honor, and virtue and innocence will eventually come out triumphant."

The problem was that none of the authorities of the law wanted to take the responsibility of releasing the prisoners. There were still too many people making trouble, and the authorities feared public opinion and, in some cases, even for their own safety.

The only solution was for the prisoners to escape. Joseph and his companions were escorted from the Liberty Jail on April 6, 1839, and taken to Daviess County. Here charges of riot, arson, burglary, treason, and receiving stolen goods were brought against them. It was dangerous for them to be tried in Daviess County, where there was so much prejudice against them. So the judge sent them on to Boone County.

With a horse-drawn wagon, some other horses, and four men to be their guards, they traveled about twenty-five miles over the next two days. When they reached their destination the second day, the prisoners bought a jug of whiskey for the guards. Most of the guards drank freely from the jug and fell asleep. One guard helped Joseph and the others saddle the horses and allowed the prisoners to escape, two mounted on horses and the others walking.

At last they were free.

It took them several days to reach Quincy, Illinois, where they found their families living in poverty. But they were all safe, and that was the thing that mattered most.

CHAPTER 27

A PLACE OF THEIR OWN

Joseph and the other brethren who had escaped from Missouri were delighted to find that the people in Illinois were friendly to them. The Latter-day Saint families who had left Missouri earlier had been treated well in Quincy. "Our state needs citizens and taxpayers," the residents said. "We welcome you to Illinois."

Many people recognized Joseph. They expressed concern and even anger about the treatment the Saints had received in Missouri. They took the Church members into their own homes and helped them find jobs. The governor of Illinois had said he would join other governors in trying to get help for the Saints from the federal government. He felt Missouri had treated the Saints in a way that violated the U.S. Constitution.

This friendliness was a pleasant relief to Joseph. But he agreed with other Church leaders that the Saints needed to find a place of their own where they could gather together as a people and build a temple, a house of God. While still in jail, Joseph had learned that land was available on a bend of the Mississippi River about fifty miles north of Quincy. Now that he was free, he could go see it.

The land included a little town called Commerce. Several dozen people who were not members of the Church already lived in the area, and there were a few businesses and homes and a post office. The land had a beautiful view of the Mississippi and the small islands in it. But much of it was overgrown with tangled underbrush and trees. It was also swampy, so swampy that horses and wagons bogged down if they tried to cross it. As Joseph and his companions walked around, they sank in mud up to their ankles.

Still, after Joseph had looked it over, he declared, "With the Lord's blessing, we can make it habitable."

Joseph and other Church leaders bought several pieces of land, including part of Commerce. They began building a new city that they named Nauvoo, which came from the Hebrew and meant "beautiful place of rest."

As the city grew, Joseph seemed to be everywhere, chopping logs, building, encouraging the people, and lifting their spirits. He worked hard, and he took time to relax. He enjoyed wrestling, running, jumping, and stick-pulling and often played ball with the young boys. Some overly serious people thought a prophet should not play such games. He answered them one day while preaching.

He told the story of a prophet who was sitting in the shade relaxing and enjoying himself, when a hunter came by with a bow and arrow.

"How can you just sit there doing nothing?" the hunter asked. "Why aren't you up and doing?"

The prophet didn't move. "Do you keep your bow strung tight all the time?" he asked.

Annoyed that he didn't seem to be answering his question, the hunter said, "No, of course not. If I did, it would lose its spring and be no good to me."

The prophet smiled. "That's the way it is with my mind. I don't want it strung tight all the time."

At the end of the story, Joseph's audience nodded in understanding and approval.

As Joseph and the others worked to turn the wilderness into a city, more and more Latter-day Saint families moved into the area. They built houses and planted crops and were pleased to discover that the soil was fertile and productive.

But now a new problem came up, a disease called swamp fever, or what we know as malaria. Many people became very ill from it, including Joseph's father, who had not been well since Joseph and Hyrum had been arrested in Missouri.

Faced with this new crisis, Joseph and Emma brought many of the sick to their home. When the house was full, they set up a tent to provide shelter for many more. Using herbs and what few medicines she had, Emma nursed them as well as she could, earning their respect and devotion.

Even Joseph, normally healthy and strong, became sick. For days, he burned with fever or shook with chills. As soon as he was well enough, he went about visiting the afflicted on both sides of the river, including Brigham Young, who had been very ill. Brigham arose from his bed healed and followed Joseph to other houses to administer to people who were sick.

One man Joseph visited was Elijah Fordham, who lay still on his bed. Joseph walked to his side and asked, "Are you very sick, Brother Fordham?" Elijah moved his head a little but could not speak.

Joseph laid his hands on the sick man's head and gave him a priesthood blessing. A few minutes later, the Prophet said to Elijah, "Brother Fordham, get up, put on your clothes, and go with me to visit some more sick people." Elijah arose from his bed and went with Joseph.

Another man, William Huntington, was so ill that he could not move or speak, although he was aware of what was going on around him. He later said he saw his friends and relatives come to his bedside and turn away, weeping. He felt that he was in the top part of the room, looking down on the weeping people and on his own body lying on the bed.

He saw Joseph and two other men come into the room. Joseph looked at him and requested a basin of water. After Joseph had washed his hands, he and the other men placed their hands on William's head and began to pray. William immediately felt that he should return to his body. He did not know how he could do this, but as Joseph said "Amen," he felt excruciating pain. Then he could see and hear and move his body again. After a moment, he sat up and swung his legs off the bed.

"You'd better be careful," Joseph cautioned. "You are very weak."

"I never felt better in my life," William replied. "I want my pants." Someone brought his clothing, and to the astonishment of all present, he walked over to sit by the fireplace. "Could I have something to eat, please?" he asked.

Everyone there knew they had witnessed a miracle.

Wilford Woodruff called these events "a day of God's power." Although sickness would continue to bother the Saints, and some people died, most recovered and returned to their work of building a city.

Throughout all of this, Joseph thought about what Missouri had done to the Mormons. He was determined to do something about it. He asked people to prepare letters about what had been taken away from them. He also obtained letters of introduction signed by the governors of Illinois, Ohio, and Iowa, declaring that Missouri had violated the people's rights.

"I am going to take these papers to Washington, D.C.," he said. "Right to Martin Van Buren, the President of the United States."

CHAPTER 28

A VISIT WITH THE PRESIDENT

On October 29, 1839, Joseph, Sidney Rigdon, Elias Higbee, and Porter Rockwell set out in a two-horse carriage for the nation's capital. Elias, a Church recorder, was one of the Saints who had been driven from Jackson County. Porter was a longtime friend of Joseph and one of the Church's earliest members.

The roads were deep with mud, making traveling slow. In addition, they made many stops to preach to the Saints along the way. Sidney, who had been extremely ill during the summer, was very uncomfortable. To care for him, the group picked up Dr. Robert Foster on the way.

On November 9, Joseph wrote to Emma, saying they would have to go on without Sidney. Joseph added a loving note of concern about his family. "It will be a long and lonesome time during my absence from you," he wrote, "and nothing but a sense of humanity could have urged me on to so great a sacrifice."

Leaving the carriage for Sidney, Dr. Foster, and Porter Rockwell to travel in, Joseph and Elias Higbee continued their journey by stagecoach. As they made their way through the mountains not far from Washington, the stagecoach driver stopped at an inn. Telling his passengers to wait, he went inside

Joseph and Elias Higbee continued their journey by stagecoach.

for some grog. But he had neglected to tie the horses to keep them from running off. Suddenly, startled by something, the horses started galloping down the hill with the coach full of people rattling behind them.

The passengers were terrified. One woman picked up her baby, saying she would throw him out of the window where he would be safer.

"No," Joseph said. "Hold him tight in your arms." Then, opening the door, Joseph climbed out, clinging to the side of the rocking, bouncing coach. Careful to avoid the thundering hooves of the horses, he managed to climb up onto the driver's seat. Yanking on the reins, he slowly brought the horses to a panting stop.

The trembling passengers tumbled out. As soon as they saw that no one was hurt, they hurried to thank Joseph. Among them were some members of Congress.

"That was a very heroic deed," one of the congressmen said. The other men nodded as he went on. "We'll mention it in Congress. I'm sure you'll be given some kind of public award for your courage. What is your name, sir?"

When Joseph told them his name, their faces changed.

"Aren't you the Mormon prophet?" one man asked.

"Yes, sir," Joseph said.

There was a silence before someone suggested that they had better go back to the inn. Nothing more was said about an award for courage.

Joseph and Elias reached their destination, Washington, D.C., on November 28. They spent the rest of that day finding a boarding house they could afford with the little money they had. On the morning of November 29, they went to the President's mansion. "We found a very large and splendid palace," Joseph wrote in a letter back to Hyrum, "decorated with all the fineries and elegancies of this world."

At that time it was fairly easy to get to see the President of the United States. When Joseph and Elias asked for an interview, they were taken upstairs to the President's parlor. President Van Buren greeted them graciously, inviting them to explain why they had come.

Joseph handed him the letters he had brought, written by the governors of the states and other important persons, saying that the Saints had been mistreated. After reading the first letter, the President frowned, saying, "What can I do? I can do nothing for you." He went on to explain that if he helped them, he would lose the votes of the people from Missouri.

Joseph did not let himself be discouraged. He explained that the Missouri mobs had violated the rights guaranteed to every citizen by the United States Constitution. The President listened silently, then asked several questions about the Church's teachings, which Joseph answered. When he finished, President Van Buren said, "I feel to sympathize with you on account of your sufferings. I will reconsider what I said earlier about not helping you."

During the next few days, Joseph and Elias met with various representatives of the government to seek help for the Saints. In general, they were treated well. The politicians from Illinois were friendly to them, and those from Missouri were not. Joseph hoped that the government could help the Saints get back what they had lost in Missouri.

During the Christmas recess, Joseph went by train to New Jersey and Philadelphia to speak to the Saints there. When he returned to Washington, he preached to an audience of many people. Some of them were congressmen curious about what he had to say. The next day a newspaper reporter named Mathew Davis wrote to his wife about Joseph, saying: "He is not educated; but he is a plain, sensible, strong minded man. Everything he says, is said in a manner to leave an impression that he is sincere. He is what you ladies would call a very good looking man. He is by profession a farmer, but is evidently well read."

At the end of his letter Mr. Davis said, "I have changed my opinion of the Mormons. They are an injured and much-abused people."

This seemed to be the opinion of many of the government leaders. But unfortunately they thought the request Joseph brought to them could not be settled by the federal government. They said he needed to deal with the state of Missouri. Joseph knew this was hopeless.

Vastly disappointed, Joseph left Elias Higbee in Washington and returned to Nauvoo. There he reported that the President of the United States had told them, "Gentlemen, your cause is just, but I can do nothing for you."

Unable to get the government help he needed, Joseph turned his attention to the problems of building a new city.

CHAPTER 29

A City Rises from a Swamp

Joseph was distressed and outraged that no one in Washington would help him find justice for the Saints. But back home in Nauvoo, he had to put his mind to other problems. There was a city to build, and a temple. The Missourians were demanding that Joseph return to their state to be tried for treason. And his father was dying.

Joseph Senior had been ill for some time. In September of 1840, he called together all of his children except for Katharine, whose husband was sick. He wanted to speak to them one last time. First he spoke to his wife, Lucy, saying, "Mother, do you not know, that you are the mother of as great a family as ever lived upon the earth?" But he was afraid to leave the children, who would yet face many troubles. After speaking to Hyrum, he turned to Joseph and said, "Hold out faithful, and you shall be blessed, and your children after you. You shall live to finish your work."

"Oh, father," Joseph cried, "shall I?"

His father nodded weakly. "You shall lay out the plan of all the work that God requires at your hand. Be faithful to the end. This is my dying blessing on your head."

After he had spoken with each of his children who were present, he had a few more words to say to Mother Lucy. Then, exhausted, he lay quietly for a time. Suddenly he remarked, as if surprised, "I can see and hear, as well as ever I could." He paused again for a few minutes. Finally he whispered, "I see Alvin." A few minutes later, he died. He was sixty-nine years old, still tall and straight but wasted to a skeleton from his long illness.

They buried him the next day. There was little time to spend in mourning. It was urgent that Joseph get to the business of making Nauvoo a place where he and the other Saints would be safe from people who might try to harass them and violate their rights, as they did in Missouri. In addition, converts were pouring into the city, not only from the states but also from overseas where Joseph had sent missionaries. They needed jobs, food, clothing, and houses.

Under Joseph's guidance, the city began to take shape. Working with other leaders, Joseph helped direct what needed to be done. Among other things, they applied to the state government for a city charter and a university. They also obtained permission to establish their own militia, which they named the Nauvoo Legion.

What pleased Joseph most was that a temple site was chosen and the work of building it begun. The temple was to be built of gray limestone from a quarry owned by the Saints. The plans called for it to be 128 feet long and 88 feet wide, with a tower on top rising to 165 feet. Joseph, through revelation, was beginning to teach the Saints about the sacred ceremonies that would take place within its walls, including baptism for the dead.

On April 6, 1841, the cornerstone was laid. To celebrate, the city sponsored a big parade, with Joseph, the Legion's commanding officer, leading it off astride a prancing horse. He wore a uniform patterned after the United States Army dress uniform, with a blue jacket and gold braid. On his head he wore a hat decorated with ostrich feathers. Twelve men with white uniforms rode with him as personal bodyguards.

Along with building the temple and all his other heavy responsibilities, Joseph took time out to greet new people as they arrived in the city. He shook hands and spoke with as many as he could, including the children. One day in the spring of 1841, Joseph was meeting with some of the newly arrived Saints in a small log house near their camping place.

During the meeting, Joseph sat quietly, his head drooping down as if he were thinking deeply. He had been silent for some time when one of the men in the meeting challenged him. "Brother Joseph," the man said, "why don't you hold your head up and talk to us like a man?"

Joseph looked up, and then turned to gaze out at the landscape. "Do you see that field of ripening grain?" he asked.

The man nodded.

"Do you see how some heads of grain are bent low?" Joseph said. "They are bent by the weight of the valuable store inside them. Now look how others, which contain no grain at all, stand very straight."

Joseph's wisdom impressed the Saints.

Tragedy struck the Smith family again in August of 1841 when Joseph's brother Don Carlos became ill and died at the age of twenty-five. In September Joseph and Emma's youngest son, also named Don Carlos, died too. He was one year old. This was a time of deep mourning, a time that helped focus Joseph's thoughts on baptism for the dead.

As the days passed, Joseph continued to be plagued by his enemies, who used any reason they could find to harass him.

On the other hand, he was loved by multitudes of people because of his kindness and concern for them. One of the many incidents of his caring was told by a man named James Leech. He had come to Nauvoo as a boy with his sister and her husband, Henry, who had joined the Church in England. James did not consider himself worthy to be baptized, but he came anyway. When they got to Nauvoo, however, they couldn't find jobs.

"Let us go and see the Prophet," James suggested.

After thinking about it a while, Henry agreed. But he was reluctant to ask the Prophet for a job. So James, although he was not a member, did so.

"Mr. Smith," he said, when they found Joseph working in a little store, "if you please, have you any employment you could give us both, so we can get some provisions?"

Joseph looked them over with a smile. "Well, boys, what can you do?"

They told him what they had done in England.

"Can you make a ditch?" Joseph asked.

They said they thought they could.

Picking up a measuring tape, Joseph said, "Come along with me." He took them to a spot near the store, and after giving James one end of the tape, he stretched it full length.

"Now, boys," Joseph said, "can you make a ditch three feet wide and two and a half feet deep along this line?"

"We can do our best," James replied. James and Henry went to work. It was hard and sweaty work, but eventually they finished it. When they told Joseph it was done, he came to see it.

Nodding his approval, he said, "Boys, if I had done it myself it could not have been done better. Now come with me."

He led them to the store. "In return for your labor," he said, "I want you to pick the best ham or piece of pork to take home with you."

Suddenly feeling bashful, James said they would rather he pick out something for them.

Joseph selected two of the biggest and best pieces of meat, then threw in a sack of flour for each of them.

"Will that do?" he asked.

"Oh, sir, that's too much," James said. "We will do more work for all of that."

Joseph shook his head. "If you are satisfied, boys, I am," he said.

They went home rejoicing. Not long after, James joined the Church.

But things didn't always go well for Joseph. A serious complication came in May of 1842 when someone tried to assassinate Governor Boggs of Missouri. Immediately the cry went up that Joseph was responsible, even though he was in Nauvoo that day, hundreds of miles away. His accusers said he must have urged Porter Rockwell to do it.

By September 1, Joseph had gone into hiding. He wrote to the Saints in Nauvoo, explaining that he had to leave "for a short season, for my own safety and the safety of this people." He assured them, "When I learn that the storm is fully blown over, then I will return to you again." He gave them instructions about recording baptisms for the dead. "And as for the perils which I am called to pass through," he wrote, "they seem but a small thing to me, as the envy and wrath of man have been my common lot all the days of my life."

To keep safe, Joseph went with John Taylor and others to stay with Brother Taylor's father for a few days on the Henderson River northeast of Nauvoo. Joseph then sent some of the men back to Nauvoo to see what was happening. While they were gone, Joseph spent his days with John's nineteen-year-old brother, William.

"The Prophet and I spent most of our time during the day in the woods, near our house walking around, shooting squirrels, or doing anything we could to amuse ourselves," William later said.

While relaxing with William, Joseph thought a lot about temple work. He sent another letter to Nauvoo about baptism for the dead. "That subject," he wrote, "seems to occupy my mind and press itself upon my feelings the strongest, since I have been pursued by my enemies."

Joseph remained in hiding from his enemies for some time. Finally, after Christmas, he traveled to Springfield, the capital of Illinois, to appear in court. The court found the papers for arresting Joseph to be faulty and ordered that he be released.

He was happy to be free, but a few weeks later, he learned that his friend Porter Rockwell had been arrested and put into a Missouri jail. Porter's mother said he needed money to help him win his freedom. Joseph worked hard to raise money to help his friend.

In order to get the necessary amount, Joseph asked a man named Thomas Colborn to loan him $100. Many years later, Brother Colborn's daughter, Sarah, told what happened. She said the Prophet told her father that he would return to repay the money in three days, if he was alive.

Sarah's Aunt Katie, who lived with the family, was angry with Thomas, and in front of the children said, "Don't you know, Thomas, you will never see a cent of that money again."

Sarah's father said, "Don't worry, Katie. If he cannot pay it, he is welcome to it."

Sarah wondered if Joseph really would return the money. She had faith that he would.

Three days passed. The third day was cold and rainy. The hours went by, and Joseph did not come. Finally the family went to bed. Suddenly someone knocked at the door. When Sarah's father opened it, they saw Joseph standing there in the rain. "Here, Brother Thomas, is the money," he said.

Sarah's father invited him inside. Someone lit a lamp as he sat down at the table. In the soft light, he counted out $100 in gold.

Sarah admired that Joseph would work so hard to keep his word and later gave her testimony that he truly was a prophet of God. The money Joseph collected helped Porter to defend himself, and he was later released from jail.

As time went on, the Saints continued gathering to Nauvoo in great numbers and established a thriving and beautiful community. The swampy land was drained, and gradually brick and frame homes arose among the many log ones. The buzz of sawmills filled the air. Steamboats hooted from the river. The streets bustled with wagons drawn by plodding oxen and clip-clopping horses moving goods and people around the town. There were schools, flour mills, and factories, as well as shops where tailors, cobblers, blacksmiths, carpenters, and other craftsmen practiced their trades. Newspapers, including the *Times and Seasons,* began publication.

Nauvoo became one of the largest and busiest cities in the state. And on the hill above the Mississippi River, the walls of the Nauvoo Temple gradually began to rise toward heaven. Men worked to shape temple stones and put them in place. The temple was the focus of Joseph's thoughts and feelings because it meant families could live together forever if the necessary ordinances were performed there.

The more Nauvoo grew, however, the more uneasy its neighbors became. With so many voters, would the Mormons take over the state, or at least the county, and run it as they pleased? Would they use the Nauvoo Legion to force others to do their will? Would Joseph Smith become so powerful that he would run for governor, or even the President of the United States? Rumors about the Saints spread rapidly in the neighboring towns.

One man who lived nearby wrote a letter regarding the Saints, saying, "They must and will take the world. And if they cannot do it by preaching, they will by the force of arms." Just as Moroni had prophesied, people spoke both good and evil of Joseph.

Nauvoo became one of the largest and busiest cities in the state.

CHAPTER 30

AN OUTRAGEOUS ARREST

In June of 1843 Joseph decided that he should take Emma away from Nauvoo for a while. Joseph arranged to go with her and their children—Julia, young Joseph, Frederick, and Alexander—many miles north to visit her sister.

Less than a week after they left, Hyrum learned that two officers, one from Missouri and another from Illinois, were coming to take Joseph back to Missouri for trial on an old charge. They had received permission from the governor of Illinois to do this.

Hyrum asked two of Joseph's faithful friends, William Clayton and Stephen Markham, to hurry to where Joseph was and warn him before the officers found him. They rode off as fast as their horses could go. They traveled 212 miles in 66 hours, hardly stopping to eat or sleep. When they finally found Joseph, he assured them he wasn't afraid. "I shall find friends," he said, "and the Missourians cannot hurt me."

He did have friends who were watching out for him, but when the two officers came into town, they were disguised as Latter-day Saint elders. They found their way to the house where Joseph and his family were staying. When someone came to the door in answer to their knock, they asked politely, "Where is the prophet? We must see him."

They were told he had gone outside. They hurried to the barnyard. Seeing him there, they strode up and jabbed their pistols into his ribs.

Outraged, Joseph demanded, "What's the meaning of this?"

"I'll show you the meaning," one of the men snarled. "If you stir one inch, I'll shoot you."

"Go ahead and shoot," Joseph mocked. "I have endured so much oppression, I am weary of life. Kill me, if you please."

"Don't give us any trouble," the man growled. "Get into the wagon." He gestured toward the wagon he and his companion had been riding in.

Joseph stood his ground. "I am a strong man," he said, "and with my own natural weapons could soon level both of you. But if you have any legal process to serve, I am at all times subject to law and shall not offer resistance."

The men did not show him any legal papers for his arrest. Instead, they forced him at gunpoint to get into their wagon.

Stephen Markham, who had come out of the house, objected. Grabbing the bridles of the horses, he yelled, "No law on earth requires a lawman to take a prisoner without his clothes." Although the officers threatened to shoot him, Stephen held onto the horses until Emma had a chance to bring Joseph's hat and coat. The men allowed him to take them; then they lashed their horses, and the wagon rocked out of the yard.

The two officers headed for Missouri with Joseph as their prisoner. Hyrum soon received word of the kidnapping and called for volunteers to catch up with the men to make sure Joseph's rights were respected. More than 175 men rode out at top speed. They spurred their horses to keep them going when they grew tired.

It took them some time to reach Joseph and his captors. When Joseph saw them, he broke into tears of joy. "I am not going to Missouri this time," he declared. "These are my boys."

The "boys" did not try to snatch Joseph away. Instead, they took charge of the entire group and turned it back toward Nauvoo, where the people came out to welcome their Prophet to freedom.

A boy named Angus Cannon witnessed Joseph's return to Nauvoo and told about it many years later. He said that Joseph leaped up onto the ledge of the well by the side of his home. Hanging onto the timber that supported the well covering with one hand, he swung his hat with the other. "I am thankful to the God of Israel who has delivered me out of the hands of the Missourians once more," he proclaimed to the multitude of people who had come to welcome him. Angus said that Joseph's voice thrilled his entire being, and that a number of people wept for joy.

The two officers who had arrested Joseph were now prisoners themselves, and they were anxious about their own safety. Joseph promised that they would be treated much better than they had treated him. True to his word, he invited them to dinner at his home that night.

Alvah Alexander, a boy who knew the Prophet, later wrote about this event. "I remember one day I was at his home playing with his children," Alva wrote, "when he came home and brought two men. These men had been arrested for abusing Joseph. He brought them in and treated them as he would one who had never done him a wrong; gave them their dinner before he would allow them to depart. Just before they sat down to dinner he brought his children up and introduced them. Pointing to me he said: 'This is a neighbor's little boy.'"

Joseph treated the officers kindly, even though they had mistreated him. A Nauvoo court decided that the officers had taken Joseph unlawfully, as had happened so often in the past. Again his rights had been violated. The attempt to arrest him on an old charge just continued the persecution that began in Missouri. Once more, he was saddened that the federal government would do nothing to protect the constitutional rights of Church members.

His enemies saw it differently. They felt that using the Nauvoo court to release him was not fair because the people of Nauvoo protected each other.

It wasn't long before he did something else that made his enemies think that one of their worst fears might come true. With the full support of the people of Nauvoo, he became a candidate for the office of President of the United States. He felt it was the only way to call attention to their problems and assure that the rights of all people, including the Saints, would be protected.

CHAPTER 31

DANGER ALL AROUND

Joseph began his campaign for the Presidency of the United States with enthusiasm and energy. As a candidate, he could express to large groups of people his feelings about the government and how it should be run.

He prepared a platform, a list of statements saying what he would try to achieve if he were President. Among other things, he wanted to abolish slavery, which some parts of America allowed at that time. Over the course of his life, Joseph had developed great concern for slaves and other people whose freedom had been taken away.

Mary Frost was a little girl in Nauvoo when Joseph Smith was mayor of the city. Years later she related a story about a black man named Anthony who broke the law by selling liquor on Sunday. Anthony told Joseph he was trying to get enough money to buy the freedom of his child who was still a slave in the south. He had already bought his own freedom and his wife's, but he could not be happy until he'd brought their child, too, to their new home.

The man pleaded his case to Joseph, who said, "I am sorry, Anthony, but the law must be observed, and we will have to impose a fine."

The next day Joseph brought a handsome horse to Anthony. "Sell it," he said, "and use the money to purchase your child."

Anthony was most grateful for Joseph's kindness and generosity.

Besides abolishing slavery, Joseph's presidential platform proposed establishing schools in prisons so those being held there would be taught a better way of life. Joseph also spoke of lower taxes and greater equality. And he urged granting the President authority to use the army to put down mobs that took away people's civil rights.

These bold statements brought him some support even outside Nauvoo. But they stirred up people who saw him as a threat because he was a powerful man. Not only was he mayor of Nauvoo and a judge of the municipal court, but he was also lieutenant general of the Nauvoo Legion and leader of a rapidly growing church. He had many enemies, some of them even inside the Church. There were rumors that some members were dealing with the Missourians who were out to get him.

There was danger all around.

But while his enemies tried to destroy him, the Saints prayed for his safety. One time when his enemies were threatening violence, someone told him that a group of children were praying for him. "Then I need have no fear," he replied. "I am safe." With a smile, he went on his way.

Sariah Johnson was one of the children of Nauvoo. Many years later she said that she had been very impressed at how much he loved children. "But," she said, "what I remember best is that I always felt a divine influence whenever I was in his presence."

In addition to planning his Presidential campaign, Joseph continued to send expeditions to faraway regions. He wanted to find a place of peace and safety for the Saints. He said, "I hope for a place where we can have a government of our own, get up into the mountains where the devil cannot dig us out, where we can live as old as we have a mind to."

He thought of several possible future locations for the Saints. Increasingly, he looked west toward the Rocky Mountains as a home for them. "Within five years," he predicted, "we will be out of the power of our old enemies." He prophesied they would not be able to destroy him until he was ready. The Lord had promised him that.

But he also knew that his time was short and that he must hurry to complete his work. He had told the recently organized Nauvoo Relief Society, "I will not be with you long to teach and instruct you. The world will not be troubled with me much longer."

Feeling anxious, Joseph labored hard to prepare the people for the future. He trained leaders in temple ordinances. He taught the people about baptism for the dead, eternal marriage, and other work that would someday be done in the temple. He wanted to make sure the other leaders of the Church would be able to go on with the work if something happened to him. In March 1844 he called the Quorum of the Twelve together for a special meeting.

"Some important scene is near to take place," he told them. "Perhaps I will be killed. This is why I want to give to you all the keys and powers that I hold. Then I can go with all pleasure and satisfaction, knowing that my work is done."

After instructing them for some time, he began pacing the floor. In a symbolic gesture, he eased the collar of his coat down upon his shoulders, saying, "I roll the burden and responsibility of leading this Church off from my shoulders and on to yours. Now, round up your shoulders and stand under it like men; for the Lord is going to let me rest a while."

But his enemies did not let him rest. They constantly accused him of wrongdoing and hounded him with legal charges. Some said he was a fallen prophet.

Despite all of the opposition, Joseph went on preparing the Saints for whatever might lie ahead. William G. Nelson later recalled a meeting at which the Prophet said, "I will give you a key that will never rust. If you will stay with the majority of the Twelve Apostles and the records of the Church, you will never be led astray."

One afternoon in April 1844, Joseph stood to give a talk in memory of King Follett, a Church member who had died the month before. It would later be called the greatest talk of Joseph's life. Perhaps ten thousand people crowded the outdoor grove where he spoke. The grove was near the temple, which was still being built.

As Joseph stood, the wind blew. Joseph told the people to pay careful attention or they would not hear him.

The sky grew stormier, and people got frightened and began to leave. Once at an earlier meeting in Nauvoo, Joseph had dismissed the people when a storm arose. This time, Joseph asked the people to pray that the winds would stop. "I believe that your prayers shall be heard," he said.

The people did as he asked. One girl would remember what happened next. "The storm divided over the grove," she would say. "It was storming on all sides of the grove, yet it was as calm around us as if there was no sign of a storm so near by. I thought as I sat there that the Lord was speaking through Joseph."

And the Lord did speak through him. Joseph spoke of who God was, and what man may become. He gave a powerful talk, and the Spirit of the Lord touched the hearts of many people there. The faithful Saints came away knowing Joseph's enemies were wrong. One man wrote, "I have evidence enough that Joseph is not fallen."

Joseph's talk was closely connected to the temple. In May he went to the shops where men were carving stones for the temple walls. There he blessed each worker by the power of the priesthood.

But still his enemies did not stop. In June of 1844 some of them began publishing a newspaper they called the *Nauvoo Expositor.* It was filled with hateful stories about Joseph. It tried to convince readers that he was a fallen prophet.

What was Joseph to do? If he ignored the *Expositor* and let it go on being published, it could endanger Church leaders and members. It threatened to weaken the city government, as well as bring the Saints closer to being driven out of Illinois. It might also destroy any hopes Joseph had of using his Presidential campaign to strengthen the rights of the Saints and other persecuted minorities.

On the other hand, if he suppressed the newspaper, it might violate the principles he was campaigning for. He did not know which way to turn.

CHAPTER 32

"We Dare Not Come"

At meetings of the Nauvoo City Council, Joseph and others discussed the *Expositor* case. After considerable discussion, it was decided that the articles the newspaper printed were libel, which meant they were untrue and damaging to Joseph and the others they mentioned. The council declared the *Expositor* to be a public nuisance because of the libel, which was against the law.

Joseph, as the mayor of Nauvoo, directed that the *Expositor* be destroyed. The city marshal and local police carried out the order, backed up by members of the Nauvoo Legion. They smashed the printing press and burned the paper and advertisements for it.

The publishers of the newspaper left town immediately, stirring up people in other communities against the Saints. False rumors were started that another anti-Mormon newspaper would be destroyed and its editor killed. In Carthage people gathered together to condemn the Mormons for what they had done. Mobs whipped up fury wherever they could, saying the Saints must be eliminated.

Knowing there would be serious trouble, Joseph ordered the Nauvoo Legion to dig trenches and make other preparations to defend Nauvoo. He also sent a letter to Governor Ford of Illinois, explaining his actions with the newspaper. He said that the deed had been undertaken only after "a long and patient investigation." He said that the equipment had been destroyed without riot or confusion.

Governor Ford decided the situation was so serious that he needed to come to Carthage to help resolve it. From Carthage he dispatched a letter requesting that Joseph send representatives to tell the Saints' side of the story.

On June 22, Joseph's delegates met with the governor and Joseph's accusers. When Joseph's friends tried to explain what happened, their enemies treated them rudely and shouted, "That's a lie!"

After the meeting, the governor sent Joseph a message, saying, "I now express to you my opinion that your conduct in the destruction of the press was a very gross outrage upon the laws and the liberties of the people. It may have been full of libels, but this did not authorize you to destroy it."

He also said, "I have great fears that your city will be destroyed, and your people many of them exterminated." He called upon Joseph and whoever else was involved to come to Carthage and submit to yet another trial. He promised his personal protection while they were there.

Joseph was astounded when he received the governor's letter. Carefully he prepared his reply. "We would not hesitate to stand another trial according to your Excellency's wish," he wrote, "were it not that we are confident our lives would be in danger. We dare not come."

Then Joseph met with some of the other brethren to consider what to do. They could go again to Washington to lay their case before the new President, John Tyler. After a short discussion, they decided that would be useless. Then suddenly Joseph's face brightened and he said, "The way is open. It is clear to my mind what to do. All they want is Hyrum and myself. We will cross the river tonight, and go away to the West." He believed that with the two of them gone, the mobs would leave Nauvoo alone.

In the dark morning hours of June 23, Joseph, Hyrum, Willard Richards, and Porter Rockwell rowed across the Mississippi. The river was choppy and dangerous due to recent heavy rains, so the crossing tired the men. The sun was coming up by the time they made it to the Iowa shore. Staggering with fatigue, they finally reached the home of a Church member, where Joseph immediately sat down to pen a note to Emma. "Do not despair," he wrote. "I do not know where I shall go or what I shall do. May God Almighty bless you and the children."

He sent Porter Rockwell back across the hazardous Mississippi to deliver the note and tell the people of Nauvoo what was happening. When Porter got there, he saw that the city was in confusion. The people did not know whether to stay where they were and defend the city or to gather up their belongings and escape while they could. Some accused Joseph of being a coward for leaving. Emma sent Porter back to Joseph with a note begging him to return and report to Governor Ford, who had promised to keep him safe.

Three men re-crossed the river with Porter. They encouraged Joseph to return to Nauvoo. They said that if he didn't, the city could be attacked and destroyed. One of the men complained, "You always said if the Church would stick to you, you would stick to the Church. Now trouble comes and you are the first to run."

These words cut Joseph to the heart. He shook his head sadly. "If my life is of no value to my friends," he said, "it is of no value to me."

Turning to Hyrum, he said, "Brother Hyrum, you are the oldest. What shall we do?"

"Let us go back and give ourselves up," Hyrum said.

"We shall be butchered," Joseph protested. But he agreed to go.

Though Joseph had fled Nauvoo with a desire to escape his enemies, when he had a chance to calm his mind, he felt the Spirit whispering to him, "Go back."

The anxious men rowed to the Illinois side of the river. Joseph spent the night with Emma and their children. He knew that this might be the last time they would ever be together in this life.

Early the next day, June 24, Joseph, Hyrum, and several other men accused of taking part in the destruction of the *Expositor* mounted their horses and started for Carthage. It was a bright summer day, with the morning sun lighting up the unfinished temple. Joseph stopped to look at it as they topped a rise in the road. He gazed, too, at the pleasant houses the Saints had built and at the gardens and orchards they had planted in what had once been a swamp. "This is the loveliest place and the best people under the heavens," he said. "Little do they know the trials that await them."

Then, turning his face toward Carthage, he said, "I am going like a lamb to the slaughter."

CHAPTER 33

CARTHAGE

Although Joseph knew he faced almost certain death in Carthage, he was calm as he and the other brethren rode toward the city. "I have a conscience void of offense towards God, and towards all men," he said. "I shall die innocent, and it shall yet be said of me—he was murdered in cold blood."

They were within a few miles of Carthage when they were met by a company of militia on horses. Their commanding officer, Captain Dunn, handed Joseph a message from Governor Ford. It instructed Joseph to order the Nauvoo Legion to give up whatever firearms had been issued to them by the state. Though the order was unfair and would weaken the Saints' defenses, Joseph agreed to it. Obeying the order would prove their cooperation with the governor. Joseph even rode back to Nauvoo with Captain Dunn and the militia so that the Legion would not resist.

Under his direction, they gave up three small cannons and about two hundred guns. Captain Dunn was surprised since rumors claimed they had many more than that. But the rumors were exaggerated.

Once again Joseph said good-bye to his family.

The Saints were uneasy about giving up the guns because they remembered what had happened in Missouri when they had received orders to disarm. But they had to trust that Governor Ford would keep the peace. Besides, Captain Dunn told them he would protect them as long as they continued to behave peaceably.

It was almost midnight when Joseph, Hyrum, and fifteen other Mormon leaders rode into Carthage with Captain Dunn and the militia. They were all exhausted, especially Joseph and Hyrum, who had not had much sleep for several days. Even though it was very late, an unruly crowd of men was waiting for them. The crowd had been drinking liquor and brawling all day, and they hooted and jeered as Joseph and the others rode through the streets. "We've got you now, old Joe," they screeched.

Captain Dunn had a hard time escorting the prisoners safely to the hotel where they would be temporarily held. The mob swarmed around, cursing and shrieking demands that Joseph be released to them. A nervous Governor Ford tried to calm them down.

"I know your great anxiety to see Mr. Smith, which is natural enough," he shouted, his thin voice scarcely heard above the noise. "I assure you, gentlemen, you shall have that privilege tomorrow morning as I will cause him to pass before the troops upon the square, and now I wish you to return to your quarters."

The mob seemed satisfied with that and began to break up.

Early the next morning, Joseph, Hyrum, and the others who had been accused surrendered officially to a local constable. Governor Ford again assured them that they would be protected. Then he had Joseph and the others taken to the public square. Climbing onto a table, he spoke to the assembled crowd.

"The prisoners are dangerous men," he said, trying to please the people, "and guilty of all that might be alleged against them. But they are now in the hands of the law, and the law must take its course."

Instead of calming the mob, these words inflamed them. When Governor Ford had the prisoners pass before the troops, some of the militiamen became infuriated because Joseph was introduced respectfully as "General Smith." They tossed their hats into the air, hissed, groaned, and threatened Joseph with guns and swords.

Joseph was saddened by how much they hated him. He would later tell the other brethren, "I have had a good deal of anxiety about my safety since I left Nauvoo, which I never had before when I was under arrest." Still, he felt the truth was on their side. In a letter to Emma that day, he wrote, "When the truth comes out we have nothing to fear. We all feel calm and composed."

In the late afternoon the prisoners had a hearing before a justice of the peace, an active anti-Mormon. The charge was that they had destroyed the *Nauvoo Expositor* in the midst of a riot. They were released with a promise that they would return to be tried later. Although most of the men left for Nauvoo, Joseph and Hyrum remained behind to talk briefly with Governor Ford.

A few hours after they had returned to the hotel for the night, they learned they were accused of treason against the state of Illinois, a very serious offense. Now instead of being free to go, they were taken immediately to the Carthage Jail, stalked by the hooting, drunken mob.

The jail was a two-story stone building with a first-floor room for people who couldn't pay their debts. On the second floor was a high-security cell for more dangerous criminals. The building also had other rooms where the jailer and his family lived. The jailer soon figured out that the Smiths were not dangerous. So he let them have a bedroom on the second floor with unbarred windows and a door that didn't lock. The room was furnished only with some chairs and a bed.

Several friends were granted permission to stay with them for the night.

The next morning Joseph asked to see Governor Ford. The governor honored the request and came to the jail. They had a friendly but serious discussion in which the governor pointed out that destroying the *Nauvoo Expositor* violated freedom of the press. Joseph explained the circumstances around what they had done. Speaking of the newspaper and what was printed in it, he said, "It was a flagrant violation of every principle of right. And it was abated on the same principle that any nuisance, stench, or putrified carcass would have been removed."

The governor appeared to express sympathy for their position and said he hoped they would be found not guilty.

Before the governor left, Joseph told him he had heard that the governor planned to go to Nauvoo the next day. Governor Ford admitted he was going to do that.

"But my brother and I will not be safe if you leave Carthage," Joseph protested.

"Then I'll take you with me when I go," the governor promised.

That night the prisoners were awakened by a gunshot. The next morning Joseph sent Dan Jones, one of the friends who had remained with him and Hyrum, to see if he could learn what the shot meant.

Downstairs the militia on guard duty told Dan, "We had too much trouble to bring old Joe here to let him ever escape alive, and unless you want to die with him you had better leave before sundown. You'll see that I can prophesy better than Old Joe."

Dan hurried off to tell Governor Ford about this threat. On his way he heard a militiaman speaking to a crowd. "When the governor and his troops have left for Nauvoo," the man said, "we will return and kill those men, if we have to tear the jail down."

The mob cheered.

Dan reported this to Governor Ford, who told him, "You are unnecessarily alarmed. The people are not that cruel."

Dan asked that the governor replace the guards at the jail. "If you don't," he said, "I have only one prayer–that I will live to testify that you have been warned."

After Dan came back to the jail and told what he had learned, Joseph wrote a letter to Emma. "I am very much resigned to my lot, knowing I am justified, and have done the best that could be done," he wrote. "Give my love to the children and all my friends. And as for treason, I know that I have not committed any, and they cannot prove anything of the kind."

Later, the prisoners learned that the governor had indeed left for Nauvoo without taking Joseph and Hyrum as he had promised. Before he left, he ordered the militias to disband, except for the troops that were left to guard the jail.

Most of the militia followed the governor's orders. They were tired of the whole matter and wanted to go home. But a few troublemakers remained behind. Disguising themselves by smearing mud and gunpowder on their faces, they headed for Carthage Jail.

Back at the jail, a friend managed to smuggle in a loaded six-shooter for Joseph's protection. Joseph had another gun, which he handed to Hyrum.

"I hate to use such things or see them used," Hyrum said.

Joseph's face was somber. "So do I. But we may have to defend ourselves."

All of Joseph and Hyrum's companions had been ordered to leave the jail. Two of them, John Taylor and Willard Richards, refused to go, preferring to remain with Joseph and Hyrum even though they might face grave danger. As the four men sat nervously in the sunlit room, Joseph asked John to sing. John, who had a lovely voice, chose a song that had recently become popular in Nauvoo. "A poor wayfaring man of grief hath often crossed me on my way," he sang. It was a plaintive song, revealing in its last verse that the poor wayfaring man who gives back generously for what he receives is the Savior Himself.

When John finished the song, Joseph asked him to repeat it.

Outside, men with blackened faces approached stealthily. The day being hot, the prisoners and their two friends sat close to the windows with the door to their room open to let in air. Several minutes after five o'clock, they saw members of the mob slip around the corner of the building and head for the stairs leading to their room. Sensing danger, Joseph and the others leaped for the door and slammed it shut, pressing against it because there was no lock.

Joseph and Hyrum reached for their guns. John snatched a heavy cane called the "rascal beater" that one of their friends had left behind. Willard grabbed another walking stick. They heard gunfire and footsteps as the mob rushed the stairs and pushed at the door, shouting and cursing. Hyrum and Willard leaned hard against the door, holding it tight. One of the attackers, thinking the door was locked, shot through the latch. Joseph and the others sprang back as the lead ball whizzed through the room.

Another ball pierced the wooden door, hitting Hyrum in the face. From outside, a second ball came blasting through an open window and ripped through his body. Falling onto his back, Hyrum cried, "I am a dead man!"

Joseph crouched over him. "Oh my poor, dear brother Hyrum!" he exclaimed. Then, rising, Joseph strode to the door, opened it slightly, and fired the six-shooter into the hallway. Only three of the six shots fired. But this was enough to make the mob pull back for a moment.

Soon the mobbers surged forward again, forcing the door partly ajar and shoving their muskets and bayonets through the opening. Joseph stepped back, and John used his cane to knock down the gun barrels. Willard, who was caught between the door and the wall it opened against, could not safely reach the guns with his stick.

The intruders' guns belched lead and fire into the room. More and more members of the mob scrambled up the stairs and jostled toward the door. Joseph, John, and Willard could not hold them back. "It looked like certain death," John would recall later. Their only hope was to leap from the open second-story window.

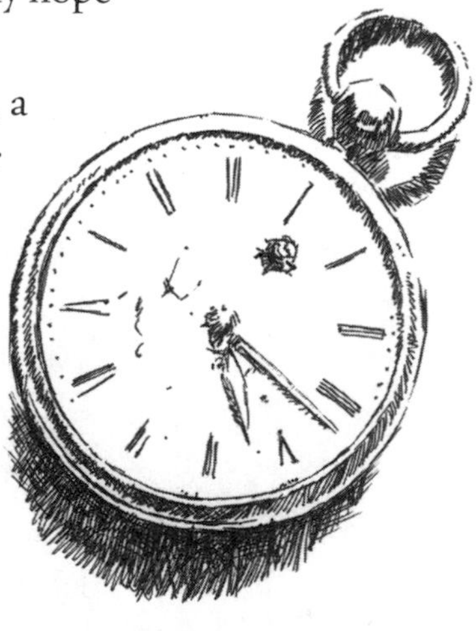

John tried first, but as he reached the window, a musket ball struck his thigh, paralyzing him briefly. For a moment he teetered helplessly on the windowsill. Then he tumbled back onto the floor. A force struck his vest pocket, smashing his watch and stopping it at sixteen minutes past five.

John collapsed on the floor and crawled under the bed. Before the firing stopped, three more balls wounded him. One hit just below his left knee. A second ripped through his forearm and wrist, lodging in his hand. The third blew a hole the size of a man's hand in his hip, splattering the wall with flesh and blood.

Meanwhile, Joseph had moved to the corner where Willard, protected by the door, desperately beat at the guns with his stick. The mobbers maneuvered their guns around the edge of the door and fired, nearly hitting the two men.

His gun empty, Joseph threw it down and vaulted toward the window. As he sprang to the sill and tried to scramble over it, he was jolted by two shots, one from the door and one from outside. For just a moment he hung there before tumbling to the ground below, crying "Oh Lord, my God," as he fell.

Someone yelled, "He's leaped the window." The men who had been coming up the stairs hurtled back down.

Willard Richards, who was unhurt except for a grazed ear, pulled the badly wounded John Taylor into the little cell next door and covered him with a mattress. "I'm sorry I can't do better for you," he whispered, "but maybe this will hide you. I want you to live to tell the story." He knew the mob would come back upstairs soon and thought surely they would kill him. But perhaps they would not see John, hidden as he was by the mattress.

When the mob did come back, they found only Hyrum's body. Willard and John were in the cell next door, but before the mobbers could look in there, someone shouted from below that the Mormons were coming. Although this was not true, the rabble fled.

The attack had lasted less than three minutes.

Outside, Joseph, the Prophet, lay dead.

CHAPTER 34

THE SECRET GRAVES

Joseph and Hyrum returned to Nauvoo for the last time on June 28, 1844. Their blood-soaked bodies had been placed in hastily built coffins and loaded onto two wagons. Their younger brother, Samuel, pale and ill with grief, drove one wagon. A friend drove the other, and Willard Richards, haggard from the events of the previous days, rode alongside. Eight mounted militia men came along as escorts to assure their safety.

John Taylor, badly injured, was left behind under the care of a doctor.

Nobody spoke. The only sound was the rattle of the wagons and the horses' hoofbeats, muffled by the mud of the rain-soaked road. The thoughts of each man were with the burdens carried on the wagons. Joseph and Hyrum, big men, strong and handsome, were dead. Joseph was thirty-eight years old, Hyrum forty-four.

Carthage was in a panic that morning. Many people loaded their belongings on wagons and fled. They expected the Nauvoo Legion to sweep into the city to avenge the deaths of their leaders. Governor Ford learned of the killings on the way back from his trip to Nauvoo. When he reached Carthage, he promised to investigate what had happened. He then warned the people of Carthage to flee the city, and he hurried away with them. Carthage became like a ghost town, deserted and desolate.

The citizens of Nauvoo were stunned when they received the dreadful news of the murders. Many walked out to meet the wagons carrying Joseph and Hyrum home. They wept and moaned. Some were angry, others too weighted down with grief to think about fighting back.

Thousands of people had gathered by the time the sad little wagon train reached Nauvoo. They stood about in the streets while Joseph's and Hyrum's bodies were taken inside Joseph's home to be washed and dressed. Willard Richards climbed onto a high place nearby and asked the crowd to be peaceful. "Trust in the law for redress," he said. Then, knowing how often the law had failed them, he added, "And when the law fails, call upon God to avenge us of our wrongs."

Neither Mother Lucy nor the wives of the murdered men were allowed to see the bodies until they were made presentable in clean, spotless clothing. Even so, viewing them was such a shock that Emma, who was expecting a baby, had to be carried to her room.

New coffins were prepared. The insides were lined with white fabric. Black velvet was spread over the bodies and held in place with brass nails. Small glass windows in the lids let people see the faces of Joseph and Hyrum. The coffins were put inside pine boxes, which served as vaults.

The next morning, the citizens of Nauvoo were allowed to come into the house to view their martyred leaders. All day people filed slowly through the house, pausing beside the coffins to express their grief. At 5:00 P.M. the viewing ended and the house was cleared so family members could pay their last respects to the Prophet and his brother.

Now preparations were made for a secret burial. Since the Missourians still advertised a price for Joseph's head, his family did not dare to bury him in a public place lest his body be dug up and mutilated. Instead, the coffins were taken out of the pine boxes and hidden in a bedroom. The pine boxes were then filled with bags of sand and nailed shut. Then the boxes were taken by wagon to the cemetery and buried after a public ceremony conducted by Church leaders.

A few hours later, in the dark of night, the coffins with the bodies inside were carried south across the street to where the Nauvoo House was being built. Here they were buried in the basement of the unfinished building. The ground over the graves was smoothed and covered with rocks, wood, and rubbish by the families and leaders so that no one else would know where they were. A heavy rainstorm that night helped erase evidence of the graves.

A few months later Emma had the coffins taken to a secret spot near the first home she and Joseph had occupied in Nauvoo. There they remained in unmarked graves until 1928, when they were moved next to where Emma was buried.

Among those most affected by the Prophet's death were the children who had known and grown to love him. Some later recorded their feelings. "I was deeply affected," wrote Alvah Alexander, "as my love for the Prophet was great. As a boy, my testimony that Joseph Smith was a true Prophet was as strong as it is now as a man; and I verily testify that Joseph Smith was a true Prophet of the living God." Calvin Moore echoed those feelings. "When I was a small boy," he said, remembering Joseph, "my impression of him was that he was a great man and a Prophet of God, and when I grew up, I got a testimony for myself, and I can say that I know he was a prophet of the living God."

John Taylor, who eventually recovered from the wounds he received on the day Joseph died, penned a tribute to the martyred Prophet. In it, he testified to people everywhere, "Joseph Smith, the Prophet and Seer of the Lord, has done more, save Jesus only, for the salvation of men in this world, than any other man that ever lived in it. He lived great, and he died great in the eyes of God and his people; and like most of the Lord's anointed in ancient times, has sealed his mission and his works with his own blood."

About the Authors

Richard E. Turley Jr., managing director of the Family and Church History Department of The Church of Jesus Christ of Latter-day Saints, oversees the Church Archives, the Church History Library, the Family History Library, the FamilySearch Center, the Granite Mountain Records Vault, the Museum of Church History and Art, various computer teams, and worldwide microfilming operations. Besides writing on Church history and family history subjects, he serves as an editor for *The Papers of Joseph Smith* series, general editor of *The Journals of George Q. Cannon,* a member of the executive committee of the Joseph Fielding Smith Institute for Latter-day Saint History at Brigham Young University, and president of the Genealogical Society of Utah. He and his wife, Shirley Swensen Turley, are the parents of six children.

Lael Jensen Littke grew up in Mink Creek, Idaho, and graduated from Utah State University. Following her marriage to George C. Littke, she accompanied him to New York City, where both sought higher education. When they moved to California, she studied writing at Pasadena City College and UCLA, later teaching extension writing classes at both institutions. She made her first story sales to Church magazines, then went on to publish in national magazines. After selling stories to *Seventeen, Boy's Life,* and the *Friend,* she decided she wanted to concentrate on writing books for young people. She now has more than thirty books to her credit, put out by both national publishers and Deseret Book. *Stories from the Life of Joseph Smith* is her first nonfiction work. Now a widow, she lives with four cats in Pasadena, California. She has one married daughter, Lori.